CONCEPTUAL TRANSFER IN THE BILINGUAL MENTAL LEXICON

Sherif Okasha

Order this book online at www.trafford.com
or email orders@trafford.com

Most Trafford titles are also available at major online book retailers.

Printed in the United States of America.

ISBN: 978-1-4669-1913-6 (sc)
ISBN: 978-1-4669-1914-3 (e)

Trafford rev. 03/20/2012

www.trafford.com

North America & international
toll-free: 1 888 232 4444 (USA & Canada)
phone: 250 383 6864 ♦ fax: 812 355 4082

Contents

Acknowledgements

I would like to acknowledge, first of all, my debt and deep gratitude to Trafford Publishing House for availing me of the unique experience of having my first book published. Special thanks are due to Jacky Valle, Trafford Publishing coordinator, for her diligent efforts and valuable advice throughout the publishing process and Kris Paris, my publishing consultant, for her decent approach. Thanks are also due to Nick Arden, Publishing Service Associate for his professional monitoring of the production process.

My heart-felt gratitude goes to my mentor and friend, Prof. Nabil Ali, the well-known authority on Arabic NLP, whose valuable encouragement and mentoring during the writing process were instrumental in continuing the project to its completion. Warm regards are due to my friend and editor Emily Benko, whose stylistic native talents spared me many rhetorical mishaps.

I would also like to extend my thanks to my subjects, both Arabic and English native speakers and translators who did not spare any time and were very patient and cooperative during the experiments.

Special thanks are due to my dear friends Ahmed Saad, Ahmed Samy, Doaa Embabi, Ahmed Salah, Waseem A. Haleem A. Hawary and Mahmoud Ghareeb for their continuous help and support.

Last but by no means least I would like to thank my family for their love and understanding all the time.

Preface

There is already a plethora of research on the mental lexicon, an interdisciplinary field of linguistic inquiry which incorporates lexicography, psycholinguistics, neurolinguistics and computational research on the representation and processing of words in the mind. The bilingual mental lexicon is a new subdiscipline of the mental lexicon which represents a common ground between studies on bilingualism and those related to the mental lexicon. Most of the research in the bilingual mental lexicon is dedicated to language acquisition and very little attention is dedicated to translation. Likewise, while concrete concepts, real-world ones, dominate the study of concepts in cognitive psychology, abstract concepts receive relatively little interest from researchers due to their so-called fuzziness and the difficulty of subjecting them to empirical observation. This study aims to fill in these research gaps and challenge the difficulties surrounding them by investigating abstract concepts and their nominal realizations in the bilingual mental lexicon of English-Arabic translators. It falls into five chapters and a conclusion.

Chapter one reviews the different approaches to both the mental lexicon and the bilingual mental lexicon and provides a definition for the basic terms in the study: the mental lexicon, the bilingual mental lexicon, abstract nouns, conceptual and lexical transfer.

Chapter two traces the philosophical, logical and psychological origins of the theory of concepts and reviews different theories of concepts and their relevance to the subject of the study.

Chapter three provides a rehabilitation of the classical view of concepts from a cognitive as well as a semantic point of view. It also proposes a model for analyzing the semantic content of concrete concepts and uses this model by analogy in the study of abstract concepts. In chapter four the basic bilingual and monolingual hypotheses on which the study is based are laid down and the methodology used in their verification is established. Chapter 4 also defines abstract concepts, proposes a typology of these concepts and discusses the interrelationship between abstract concepts and abstract nouns. It applies the same methods used in analyzing the internal structure of concrete concepts to abstract concepts.

Chapter five discusses the results of experiments conducted with monolingual subjects of both languages and bilingual subjects who are English-Arabic translators. The aim of these experiments is to find out the way abstract concepts are processed in the monolingual minds of Arabic and English native speakers and the bilingual mind of English-Arabic translators. A correlation between the autonomous monolingual level and the shared bilingual level is hoped to bring to light some semantic universals as far as the conceptual structure is concerned.

Chapter six explores the impact of the process on the product. It examines how the model of conceptual processing of abstract nouns in the translator's bilingual mental lexicon can be applied in the analysis of the translational equivalents of these nouns in translated texts. A sample bilingual corpus of 4000 words, selected from the United Nations English-Arabic bitexts, is used in the analysis of translation equivalents.

Chapter 1

Review of Literature

1.1 The mental lexicon

Since the term *mental lexicon* was ever coined by Oldfield in 1966, there have been scores of studies trying to answer questions related to what exactly the mental lexicon is, how words are arranged and processed inside our minds and whether words are the be-all and end-all representations in the lexical mind or there is a deeper underlying level of psychological representations. These studies are interdisciplinary in scope, incorporating areas of neurolinguistics, cognitive psychology, lexicology and semantics into the study of the mental lexicon. The present section surveys these studies in some detail.

1.1.1 Definition, scope and evidence

Simply defined, the mental lexicon, "to use the Greek word for dictionary is the human word-store"[1], or in other words, it is "the lexicon which each speaker carries around inside his/her head, that is to say the lexical knowledge upon which all use of any given language heavily depends"[2] A working definition has been proposed by Bonin (2003) that "the mental lexicon corresponds to the mental repository of all representations that are intrinsically related to words"[3]. He further elaborates that "the mental lexicon contains several different types of representations corresponding to words, including phonological, semantic, morphological and orthographic representations"[4] This definition lays down the psycholinguistic basis of the mental lexicon as a cognitive store of not just words but also of mental representations corresponding to words. A mental representation is defined by (Zelnick, 1990) as "the internal replication of external reality"[5]. Words represent the link between this external reality and its internal replication.

Empirical literature on the mental lexicon indicates that "The large number of words known by humans and the speed with which they can be located point to the existence of a highly organized mental lexicon"[6] Psycholinguistic experiments assert the fact that an educated adult native speaker of English is likely to know no less than 50, 000 words, which suggests that the mental lexicon is subject to some systematic arrangement[7]. Experiments have also revealed that words can be retrieved in as fast as a split second." This is apparent above all from the speed of normal speech, in which six syllables a second, making three or more words, is fairly standard"[8]

Word searches, speech errors and psycholinguistic experiments provide major clues to the mental lexicon[9]. When we try to locate a forgotten word in our memory, we usually do so by searching through closely related words, a process which gives researchers clues to the whole organization of the mental lexicon. Speech error evidence is particularly important since speech errors have been found to be rule-governed and usually follow a regular pattern. They are of two types: assemblage errors and selection errors. In the first type, items are found in the memory, yet assembled in the wrong way, as in *patter-killer* for *caterpillar* and *par cark* for *car park*. In the second type, a wrong item is selected in place of the targeted one, as in saying *capital punishment* when one targeted *corporal punishment*[10]. It is this second type of speech error which is important for the mental lexicon since it can be assumed that anyone who accidentally produces a wrong word is likely to have picked one closely related to the intended word.

Today, experimental psychology applies highly sophisticated techniques in the investigation of the mental lexicon. The most common of these are lexical decision and priming. In a lexical decision task, subjects are presented with letter and sound sequences and are asked to decide whether each sequence represents a word or non-word. Their reaction time is measured in milliseconds and is supposed to provide information as to which words are the most readily available in a person's mental lexicon.[11] In priming, the assumption is that if a word primes another . . . i.e. facilitates its processing, the two are likely to be closely connected. In the semantic priming paradigm, "target words are presented for identification in the context of related or unrelated prime words. Typically, the target is recognized more quickly when the prime is semantically related rather than unrelated"[12]

There are two types of priming: associative priming and semantic priming[13]. In associative priming, the prime is associated to the target and will call it to mind but is not semantically related to it, as in the associative pair spider-web. In semantic priming, the prime and the target are semantically similar (e.g. whale-dolphin., table-stool)

1.1.2 The mental lexicon and book dictionaries

One way to shed light on the organization and content of the mental lexicon is to compare it with book dictionaries and show the dissimilarities holding between these dictionaries and the mental lexicon[14]. Generally speaking, dictionaries are static representations of the human word-store. Words in dictionaries are organized in an alphabetical order from A to Z, while in the mental lexicon they are organized mainly on the basis of meaning. This has been demonstrated by the finding that slips of the tongue do not usually involve replacement of a word by an alphabetically adjacent word, but rather by a semantically related one, as when a speaker says "inhabitants of the car" when he wants to say "occupants of the car"[15].

With regard to content, Aitchison et al list fundamental differences between the mental lexicon and book dictionaries which can be summed up as follows:

- Data in book dictionaries is unavoidably outdated, since the vocabulary of a language is constantly undergoing changes which only the human mental lexicon can cope with. There are even new meanings created on the spur of the moment. For example, the instruction "please do a Napoleon for the camera" is readily interpreted by English native speakers to mean a Napoleon pose, i.e. with one hand tucked inside the jacket[16]

- The amount of syntactic and semantic data about each lexical entry is relatively small in book dictionaries compared to the mental lexicon[17]. For example, no paper dictionary will tell us that the verb *resemble* cannot be passivized, or that while you can say "a main road", you cannot say "the road is main".

Besides, dictionary definitions do not provide us with all the semantic features a word has in the mental lexicon. For instance, while in one dictionary the first sense of *paint* appears as "to cover with paint", one still can cover one's hands with paint, e.g. accidentally, without necessarily painting them[18]

- Words in dictionaries stand in isolation from other semantically related words. For example, while *warm* is defined in one dictionary as "of fairly high temperature", the same dictionary does not tell us how it slots into the range of temperature words such as *cold*, *tepid* and *hot*. Such kind of information is a peculiarity of the mental lexicon[19] While book dictionaries provide no clues about word frequency and word prototypicality, the mental lexicon has such clues. For example, English native speakers know that *house* is a more frequent word than *abode* and that a sparrow is a more typical bird than a pelican or a flamingo[20]

The above review, it should be noted, is not intended to shed light on the shortcomings of book dictionaries, but rather to capture the main aspects of the mental lexicon. Though electronic databases in the recent years have made possible the storage and retrieval of huge amounts of information about lexical entries, they still fall short of the mammoth structure known as the mental lexicon.

1.1.3 Representation of meaning in the mental lexicon

Representations are mental featural patterns related to the organization and content of data in the mental lexicon, whether on the lexical word-level or the underlying conceptual level. Thus; there are two levels of representation: lexical-word representations and semantic representations. Though there have been many theories in cognitive psychology about the representation of meaning in the mental lexicon, "the general idea underlying the various theories and approaches is that the various lexical units, and/or the underlying concepts are represented mentally as a set of elements or entries bearing some relations to one another"[21]. For example, Quillian (1968) assumes that words are stored in memory as configurations that point to other words, and each configuration gives a representation of the meaning of a word. Collins and Quillian (1969) maintain that concepts are connected in hierarchical networks, and the connections are used to make various category decisions. For example, to decide that a dog is an animal, according to this approach, requires one to traverse the node "mammal in the hierarchy before reaching the node for animal[22]

1.1.3.1 Conceptual approaches to the mental lexicon

A major question which the literature on the mental lexicon tries to answer is: What do words refer to?. In Referential semantics, the answer will be that words refer to objects or events in the real world, that is, the word *dog*, for instance, refers to the set of all dogs or all possible dogs that ever existed[23]. The psychological approach rejects this view on the grounds that people do not know the set of all dogs or all possible dogs. Thus, a sentence like" dogs have four legs" would never be comprehensible. Moreover, what about dogs that did not exist as in the sentence "If I had a dog, I would call it Brown" or fictional dogs?. It becomes obvious, then, that the referential theory of meaning is not adequate as a psychological theory.

As an alternative, the psychological approach assumes that "people have some sort of mental description that allows them to pick out examples of the word and to understand it when they hear it"[24]. In our present example, I can understand the word *dog* when I hear it since I can retrieve my description of what *dog* means in my mental lexicon. This mental description is the concept I have in mind about dogs. A concept is defined by Murphy (2004) as "a nonlinguistic psychological representation of a class of entities" and word meaning as "that aspect of words that gives them significance and relates them to the world". Words are given their significance by being connected to concepts[25]. Words are, therefore, acoustic or visual shells which overlie both conceptual and linguistic knowledge:

> One of the unique and essential properties of the acoustic or visual objects called "words" is that they provide, either directly or indirectly, access to both linguistic and nonlinguistic knowledge. The connection is bidirctional. Linguistic and/or conceptual representations can be connected with word representations that subsequently can be produced (that is, transformed into some physical realization)[26]

Bidirectionality of the word-concept relationship means that words map to concepts and each concept has a corresponding word to which it maps. This bidirectionality has been open to question since it has been found that there are concepts that do not have words to go with them. Some examples are found in the unword online dictionary:

> **Elbonics**: The actions of two people maneuvering for one armrest in a movie theatre or airplane seat.
>
> **abandonmitt** (n.) The act of abruptly letting go of someone's hand before they anticipated it.
>
> Example: She sought therapy because of her severe abandonmitt issues

Before the bold-type words were suggested people were familiar with the concepts and used them in their relevant domains.

Another issue subject to debate is whether each single word maps to a single concept or could map to two or more different concepts. There are two views reviewed by Murphy (2004): The first one assumes that the relationship between words and concepts is one to many. This means that a single word can be connected to more than one concept as in the case of homonymy. For example the word *bank* may refer to a mass of earth by the side of a river or a commercial institution. In a similar way, a single concept can be connected to more than one word, as in the case of synonymy where two synonymous words are connected to the same concept. The other view maintains that only a single word can be connected to a single concept and the ambiguity resulting from homonymy can be theoretically resolved by listing the ambiguous words twice. The problem with the first view is that it equates words with concepts while in fact there are concepts with no corresponding words, as has just been demonstrated. The second view has also been subject to criticism on the grounds that "It is not entirely clear what "one concept" is:

> If our conceptual system is a highly interconnected set of facts and beliefs (as the knowledge view suggests, for example), then picking out a single concept could be difficult, since chopping the concept away from its connections would not correctly represent how it works within the conceptual system[27]

Moreover, Murphy (2004) maintains that there are words that are connected to just part of a concept and not all of it. For example *leap* captures only the act of jumping off, but not landing[28]. Besides, in cases of polysemy, when two senses of a word are closely related, as in the two senses of *bank* as a commercial institution (*the illegal practices of banks*) and a building (*the bank was set on fire by the attackers*), the two senses point to different concepts and since they are closely related, the word *bank* cannot be listed twice in the lexicon model.

There are two conclusions we can draw from the above discussion. First, when there is a word, there is inevitably a concept, though the reverse is not necessarily true. Second, we have to be flexible about how concepts make up the meaning of a word and not adopt a hard-and-fast line, always assuming that words map to concepts in a straight one to one relationship.

There is massive empirical evidence supporting the theory of concepts as the basis of word meaning. Experiments conducted in this regard usually focus on category relations and typicality effects. It is a general observation in the experimental psychology of concepts that items belonging to the same category are more related than items belonging to different categories. Garrod and Sanford (1977) studied the comprehension of anaphoric nouns based on category relations. For example, if I'm talking about a thief, I can later refer to the same thief saying "the criminal escaped", since a thief is a kind of criminal[29]. Typical items are more easily recognized and produced than atypical ones. Rips, Shoben and Smith (1973) found that it took longer to verify a sentence like "an eagle is a bird" than "a robin is a bird", where eagle is less typical than robin.

In some priming experiments, subjects hear first a spoken word, and then see a written version. In this way, some researchers hope to gain information about a possible abstract, underlying counterpart of the word[30]

1.1.4 Lexical processing in the mental lexicon

"The representation of an item in the mental lexicon is referred to as lexical entry" and "The central task of lexical processing is to gain access to the entry's lexical specification"[31]

Handke (1995) divides the processing of lexical entries in the mental lexicon into three levels: pre-lexical, lexical, and post-lexical level. The lower level of pre-lexical processing involves the perception of speech/written language; that of lexical processing is concerned with word recognition and lexical retrieval and the third level is dedicated to comprehension of both semantic and syntactic input[32] Handke suggests that the flow of information between the three levels can be defined either in terms of an "autonomy model" or an interactive model. In the autonomy model, the flow of information is bottom-up and decisions at the lower levels are not determined by information coming from higher levels. The interactive model, on the other hand, allows information flow between the processing levels in a top-dwon fashion in which levels further removed from the input influence lower levels[33].

These two models mentioned by Handke are based on the language production model suggested by Bock (1982) and Levelt (1989). According to this model, the natural language processing system has three processing levels:conceptualizing, linguistic processing and low-level processing. Thus, in an autonomy model, the processing takes a strict serial path in which low-level processing takes place before linguistic processing, linguistic processing before conceptualizing. In an interactive model, the three components operate in parallel[34]

In a stronger version of interactivity, the level of conceptualizing not only influences but constrains the level of linguistic processing[35]. In the current research, it will be shown that in language comprehension involved in a complex cognitive process such as translation, the two models interact.

Singleton (2000) makes a distinction between direct and indirect models of the processing of lexical information. In direct models, lexical access is a one-step process comparable to accessing items in a software package by typing in the first letters of an item which distinguish it from all other stored items. In an indirect model, it is assumed that lexical access involves more than one step or component; it is metaphorically likened to looking up a word in a dictionary or finding a book in a library.[36]

Direct models include: The logogen model and the cohort model. Logogen is made up of two words: Logo, the Greek term for word and gen, which is Latin and Greek for "give birth". The logogen system is based on the assumption that a word is easily recognized or "born" when used in a context in which it is very likely to occur. The logogen system is assisted by a cognitive system and a response buffer. When the information is full or reaches a "threshold" the logogen is activated and "fires" and the word is recognized in comprehension or identified for the purpose of production. The response buffer is responsible for the actual production of the word in speech or writing.

The cohort model is a lexical processing model for speech recognition developed by the British psycholinguist William Marslen Wilson. "It identifies the uniqueness point for word recognition, that is, the precise point at which a word is recognized" For example, in the recognition of the spoken word *elephant*-the cohort of word-candidates would include words such as *elevate* and *element*. However, at the point where the /f/ sound occurs the cohort will have only *elephant* and its inflectional variants: (elephants, elephant's, elephants') left, since no other word in English begins with the sequence /3lif/. This then is the uniqueness point for elephant.

Forster's model of lexical processing represents an indirect model of lexical access. This model is based on the idea that words in the mental lexicon are accessed in two steps: the first step involves accessing peripheral access files each of which contains initial information corresponding to the kind of lexical process involved: an orthographical access file in the case of writing, a phonological access file in the case of listening and a syntactico-semantic file in the case of word production. Then the processing goes to the deeper-level of accessing the master-file in which meaning connections between items are provided for. Such connections make processing easier through semantic priming, for example. However, there is no sufficient experimental evidence in psychology to support this model[37].

1.2 The bilingual mental lexicon

The bilingual mental lexicon is a general term for the bilingual word-store of speakers of two languages, be they native speakers of these two languages, just one of them or nonnative speakers of them both. Studies of the bilingual lexicon are mainly concerned with how words are acquired by bilinguals and language learners in general and how lexical items are processed in their minds. However, they give us some clues to similar processes in the minds of a special category of bilinguals, namely, translators. Therefore, a selective review of such studies is essential as a preliminary step to approach the translator's bilingual mental lexicon.

1.2.1 Definition, scope and evidence

The bilingual mental lexicon is an interdisciplinary area which combines both practical and theoretical issues related to the representation and processing of word meanings in bilinguals and cross-linguistic influences between languages. Studies in the field of the bilingual mental lexicon focus mainly on bilingualism and second/foreign language acquisition, whether in a natural environment or by means of formal education and are concerned with both proficiency and productivity[38]. These studies follow a developmental pattern which tracks the development of lexical, morphological and semantic representations in bilinguals. Lexical semantics is a prime candidate of study in the bilingual mental lexicon[39]

Recent empirical research has proved that there are two separate systems involved in the representation of lexical information in the bilingual mind. It is assumed that early bilingualism is compound, that is, the two systems are not distinct from each other. As the child grows, he moves towards two separate systems of speech, which, it should be noted, is presented as being equal to bilingualism as being "ideal" and permanent[40]. In a small-scale experiment conducted by GENESEE et al (1978), it was shown how early bilinguals are more inclined to keep their two linguistic systems functionally distinct than is the case with late bilinguals.[41] The translator, as a special type of bilingual, will naturally fall into the latter category of late bilinguals, an "ideal" and "permanent" user of two languages with two distinct language systems who is capable of using them in a highly specialized way. Baetens (1986) argues that:

> Bilingualism must be able to account for the presence of
> at least two languages within one and the same speaker,
> remembering that ability in these two languages may
> or may not be equal and that the way the two or more
> languages are used plays a highly significant role[42]

There are so many typologies in the literature on bilingualism. The main, broad classifications are societal bilingualism and individual bilingualism[43]. Societal bilingualism is a situation which exists when there are two languages spoken by two different groups in a single society, while individual bilingualism simply refers to the ability of using and/or the usage of two languages by a single person, with relative degrees of proficiency, whether he lives in a bilingual or a unilingual society. Of course it is individual bilingualism which concerns us in our study of the bilingual mental lexicon, since societal bilingualism is more relevant to the sociology of language. Within individual bilingualism, a differentiation is made between the natural or primary bilingual and the secondary bilingual[44]. A natural bilingual is one whose bilingualism has been acquired through natural contact with the two languages rather than through any formal instruction and is not in a position to translate or interpret between them.

A secondary bilingual, on the other hand, is a person whose second language has been added to a first language via instruction. To this latter category of secondary bilinguals belong most translators, since a situation where the source language is naturally acquired along with the target language is not so frequent.

We can conclude so far that the bilingual mental lexicon, in its mature and permanent form, is the repertoire of shared lexical information between two language systems in the mind of the bilingual, whether he uses them for the purpose of everyday communication or in highly complex cognitive processes such as translation.

1.2.2 Conceptual and lexical transfer in the bilingual mental lexicon

Three types of concepts can be distinguished in the bilingual mental lexicon: L1-based, L2 based and shared concepts, primarily on the basis of their links to linguistic and cultural representations in the mind, but do not constitute separate conceptual systems, or stores of knowledge[45]. This view amounts to a rejection of the traditional assumption of two separate language systems in the bilingual mind. It owes its roots to Lakoff's theory of experientialism. According to Lakoff, our conceptual system is directly influenced by our sensory experience of the real world. The nature of our perceptual capacities as well as the nature of the world determine much of the structure of our mental images. This type of forced image structure is referred to as preconceptual structure. According to him, this imposed image schematic structure allows us to fit language to our perceptions and rich images[46]. The real world thus consists of a concrete element, which is the physical environment and an abstract element, which is culture. Environmental factors and cultural conventions are conveyed to us indirectly through language.

Jarvis (1998) applied the theory of experientialism to the study of conceptual transfer in the interlingual lexicon. According to him concepts in two languages can be different relative to the image-schematic predispositions which determine the conceptual structures of the speakers of these two languages. Such differences concern both the content and organization of concepts. With regard to internal content," the closest corresponding concepts from two different languages may be associated with different basic-level (gestalt) images or image schemas, based both on differences in speakers' experiences and differences of convention[47] With regard to organization, differences in the conceptual structures underlying two different languages can be attributed to differences in everyday experience. This can be observed when we consider the fact that different languages often have different category prototypes, as in the case of many Americans identifying the robin, which is so common a bird species in the United States, as the best example of a bird, while this is not the case in many other parts of the world, where other varieties are familiar[48]

Shifting the focus to bilingualism, Jarvis concludes that L1-based concepts, L2-based concepts and shared concepts influence the bilingual's both L1 and L2 performance. In the case of advanced bilinguals, some degree of L2 influence on their use of L1 should be expected[49]

Recent empirical research in the bilingual mental lexicon has been in support of both the shared and separatist views of the conceptual structure and storage of lexical data in the bilingual mind, not only in bilingual knowledge development, but also in bilingual productivity in general.

To test the sharing of conceptual relations across translation equivalents, two experiments were conducted with bilingual Chinese subjects whose second language is English. Using the priming paradigm, the results of experiment 1 indicate "shared storage for the conceptual representations of the bilingual's two vocabularies[50] Experiment 2 examined meaning separation by eliciting semantic closeness rankings for conceptual relations that are equivalent across language translations and those that are not. The results indicate that bilinguals also maintain a separatist tendency to "maintain the L1 conceptual system in the representation of L1 words and to adopt the L2 conceptual system in the representation of L2 words"[51].

Translation tasks as such are basically psycholinguistic experiments whereby access to conceptual representations in the bilingual mental lexicon is tested. They do not involve complex processes such that is involved in transforming a whole text from L1 to L2 and are conducted on the level of lexical items in order to control for other factors related to the higher units of sentence and text so that the words, being physical realizations of the context-free concepts, may reveal the underlying characteristics of these concepts.

A central claim in the bilingual mental lexicon literature is that: "There are two different routes to translation: translation from the first language to the second language is hypothesized to be conceptually mediated, whereas translation from the second language to the first is hypothesized to be lexically mediated[52]. Empirical evidence for the two models of conceptual and lexical mediation is obtained by measuring RTs (response times) of subjects translating words from L1 to L2 and vice versa. RTs for L1-L2 translation were found to be longer than those for L2-L1 translation since in the former case the bilingual accesses the less well-known second language indirectly through a conceptual link in L2 to the translation equivalent in L1, which causes a delay in processing.[53] In the latter case, corresponding to the lexical mediation model, the translation is only word for word, that is, only lexically mediated. The concept mediation effect was obtained when the words were presented in categorized lists rather than randomized ones[54], which is considered as further evidence of the conceptual mediation hypothesis in translation from L1 to L2 since a concept is by definition a category of mental objects not a motley assortment of unrelated things. In translation theory, translation is assumed to involve both lexical and conceptual transfer equally in either direction. This will be discussed in more detail within the context of our discussion of the literature on the translator's bilingual mental lexicon.

1.2.3 Lexical processing in the bilingual mental lexicon:

Words in a bilingual's two languages prime (i.e. facilitate the processing of) each other if they are either semantically or associatively related. Semantically related words are words which belong to the same conceptual category[55]. In some studies; category membership is the defining basis of a semantic relation. For example, in a Shwanenflugel and Rey study[56] (1986), the primes were category names and the targets were category exemplars. Associatively related words, on the other hand, are usually cognates (words that share the same or similar form and meaning[57]

There are three classical approaches to the organization of words in the bilingual memory: compound, coordinate, and subordinate[58]. The compound and subordinate systems assume a single underlying conceptual system that is shared by both of the bilingual's vocabularies. In contrast, the coordinate system assumes two conceptual systems, one associated with each of the two vocabularies.

The compound system model is compatible with the conceptual mediation model and the subordinative system, also known as word association model is just another label for the lexical mediation model[59]

The most recent approach adopted by de Groot et al (1993) postulates that:

> within the lexicon of an individual bilingual all three of these representational structures may be found, the representational format of a pair of word translations depending on particular characteristics of the word and the associated concept"[60]

De Groot (1993) concludes that, based on Kroll and Curely (1988) observations that as bilinguals mature towards L2 proficiency, they switch from word association to concept mediation in both directions, that is from a subordinate to a compound system. An important factor in attaining this compounded status is the degree of similarity of the meanings in both L1 and L2." The more similar the meanings of the translations, the more likely they are to be stored compoundly in the mental lexicons of some types of bilinguals[61]

1.3 The translator's bilingual mental lexicon

An adequate theory of translation studies translation both as a process (i.e. translating) and as a product (translated texts). Investigating translation as a process requires a study of information processing while investigating it as a product requires a study of texts "not merely by means of the traditional levels of lexical analysis (syntax and semantics) but also making use of stylistics and recent advances in text-linguistics and discourse analysis"[62] The lexicon plays a central role in all translation studies both as a process and as a product (Bassnet, 2005, Baker, 2009). Cognitive approaches to the translator's bilingual word-store are concerned with the process, while lexical contrastive analysis studies focus on the product i.e. the ultimate impact of the process on the actual lexical items and their translation equivalents in real texts. The remaining sections represent a review of both approaches.

1.3.1 The translator as a bilingual

As has earlier been demonstrated, the translator is a special type of bilingual; the difference between him and the ordinary language learner being that while the latter's bilingualism is constantly in the making, the farmer's is settled, "ideal" and "permanent".

The translator is commonly defined as "a bilingual mediating agent between monolingual communication participants in two different language communities"[63]. Definitely this mediating agent will be different from the ordinary bilingual in many respects. First, while the ordinary bilingual uses his two languages alternatively, a translator uses them almost simultaneously, one for production and the other for comprehension. The ordinary bilingual has a wide range of choice as regards the use to which he puts his two languages: he may use both of them in independent situations and may come into contact with either of them for the purposes of comprehension only, production only or both. The translator, on the other hand, must employ his two languages at the same situation, decoding from the SL (comprehension) and re-encoding in the TL (production) and he must be proficient at both levels in order to deserve the denomination of translator.

Second, In the case of the ordinary bilingual, it is the communication situation which decides his choice of which of the two languages he must use in language production, while the translator is led in such a choice solely by the SL-TL directionality of the stretch of discourse being translated.

Third, in translation bilingualism, a baseline level of proficiency in both languages is required, while no such standardization is specified for the ordinary bilingual and thus the notorious relativity of bilingual proficiency remains an unsolved problem in bilingualism literature. (cf:Baetens, 1986:P.7).

If, however, we set apart the previous sociolinguistic definition of the translator as a mediating agent between monolingual participants and adopt purely linguistic and psycholinguistic approaches, we can detect several attributes common between the ordinary bilingual and the professional translator. From the psycholinguistic point of view, both experience a mental process of conceptual and lexical transfer between two languages. This process is called translation in bilingual lexicon literature, as we have seen, though translation in this sense is, for all intents and purposes, only partially related to the integrated process of written translation undertaken by professional translators.

Translation experiments carried out by experimental researchers in the field of the bilingual mental lexicon come in the form of wordlists in both L1 and L2 presented to subjects, mostly ordinary bilinguals, who are required to translate them from L1 to L2 and/or vice versa[64]. A major aim of such experiments is to test whether bilinguals have shared or separate representational systems for both L1 and L2, as has been demonstrated. However, they give us insights into what happens in the translator's bilingual mental lexicon since they shed the light on the relations lexical items in one language directly have to their translation equivalents in the other, or indirectly, through conceptual mediation. Such focusing of attention helps sharpen the emphasis on the underlying concepts as purely mental representations and the lexical items as physical realizations of these mental representations by stripping the latter of any linguistic context with a view to placing them in their psychological one. The translation theorist then can put them back into a linguistic context of their own to examine the effects and projections of cognitive processes on the final product, having, through empirical eyes, seen such effects at a vantage point beyond the reach of researchers who focus only on the product rather than the process, employing merely the tools of linguistic and lexical discourse analysis.

From both the linguistic and the pragmatic viewpoints, though the translator is more restricted than the ordinary bilingual in his choice of the language of production, once this choice is made both are in an equal position in terms of the selection of the appropriate linguistic forms, lexical and syntactical, that suit their respective communication situations.

1.3.2 The translator's bilingual mental lexicon: definition

In the psycholinguistic literature on translation, there is not such a term as "the translator's mental lexicon, or the translator's bilingual mental lexicon. However, near approximations to these concepts do exist. The nearest term to a translator's mental lexicon in translation theory is the frequent lexis store (FLS) defined as "the mental (psycholinguistic) correlate of the physical glossary or terminology database, i.e. an instant 'look-up' facility for lexical items both 'words' and 'idioms'[65]

A translator's bilingual mental lexicon would be the total of the FLS's of his two languages: "We imagine there to be one FLS and one FSS (frequent structure store) for each language the translator knows"[66]. "The incoming string is passed initially to the FSS and then to the FLS. The ordering is important, since it is not unusual for a reader to be able to parse a clause without understanding the meanings of the words in it"[67]

1.3.3 Conceptual approaches to the translator's bilingual mental lexicon

From the point of view of translation, a concept is "a bundle of meaning components"[68] which is unpacked by the translator in the analysis process and re-packed into a corresponding bundle in the receptor language in the synthesis process:

> A translator will often find that there is no exact equivalent between the words of one language and the words of another. There will be words which have some of the meaning components combined in them matching a word which has these components with some additional ones. There will be overlap, but there is seldom a complete match between languages"[69]

It is evident from the above statement that parallel to the process of lexical transfer is an underlying process of conceptual transfer in the translator's bilingual mental lexicon. In the next two sections I will review conceptual and lexical transfer in the process of translation (psycholinguistic analysis) and their projections on the product (contrastive linguistic analysis) in the light of the literature pertaining to these two areas.

1. 3.3.1 Conceptual and lexical transfer: the process

The process of translating is interpreted within the framework of human information processing[70]. Two types of entry are represented in the translator's memory: encyclopedic entry and lexical entry[71]. The encyclopedic entry is a conceptual entry which contains information related to a particular concept.

There are three types of information stored in the conceptual entry: class membership, concept characteristics and examples of the concept. Class membership information concern the IS-A links the concept has with other concepts. Information related to the characteristics of the concept concern the properties and qualities of that concept.[72] Properties are essential defining characteristics of the concept and must be present. A tiger, for example, must have legs in order to be called a tiger. There is a has-as-parts relationship between the concept TIGER and the concept LEGS. Qualities, on the other hand, are expected attributes of a concept and not defining characteristics of it. Besides, their presence could be a matter of degree: a tiger may be unfierce or more or less fierce. There is an applies-to relationship between the concept TIGER and the concept FIERCE[73]. Examples of a concept are objects in the real world to which the concept applies. Thus, there is an "instance of relationship between a particular physical tiger and the concept TIGER which allows us to classify it as belonging to this class of concepts[74]

To illustrate further, we can pick an example from abstract concepts. Let that be the concept LANGUAGE. We can speculate about the kind of information stored in the conceptual entry for LANGUAGE. The defining properties for language could be: means of communication and/or expression. Meaning can also be a defining property since all languages, even artificial languages or animal language must signify something. Syntax and phonology are expected qualities, not defining attributes since some varieties of the concept LANGUAGE, say, body language do not have a syntax. Arificial languages such as programming and mathematical languages, though they do have syntax, do not have a phonological system. Examplars of LANGUAGE stored together with this information are expected to be such LANGUAGE instances as English, Cobol and Esperanto.

The lexical entry contains two types of information: information related to componential analysis and that related to meaning postulates.[75] Componential analysis is concerned with the distinctive semantic and grammatical features which are binary in form and listed as either present or absent such as Adult+ and Male+. Meaning postulates concern the links between words in terms of their sharing characteristics-hyponomy, synonomy, antonomy. This context-bound information is stored in the episodic memory, while the conceptual entries, being context-free information, are stored in the conceptual memory[76]. In our present example of the concept LANGUAGE, we can argue that the lexical entry should include reference to words which bear a semantic relation to language, say a synonym like the noun *tongue*, or hyponyms such as English, French or COBOL.

It is clear that some information will be stored twice, both in the conceptual entry and the lexical entry. This means that the model provided by Bell (1995) cannot accommodate abstract concepts. In chapter 2 a new model will be provided for abstract concepts which integrates the lexical and the conceptual data in the content of a single representation.

Processing takes place simultaneously in a bidirectional fashion, following a top-down path from concepts to data and a bottom-up one from data to concepts[77]. (Baker (2009) differentiates between the professional translator and the nonprofessional translator as far as the directionality of processing is concerned. The strategy of the professional translator is sense-oriented, relying exclusively on top-down processing and focusing on function rather than form. He/she has a single store of encyclopedic (i.e. conceptual) entries and two distinct stores for the lexical entries of both languages. The strategy of the non-professional and student translator, by contrast, is sign-oriented, focusing on form rather than function. He/she relies more on lexical transfer whereby the sign in the target language is called up by the sign in the source language than on conceptual transfer in which the relevant concepts are called up by the words[78].

Green (1993) provides further evidence that translation is conceptually mediated in both directions. According to him, the categorization effect observed in L1-L2 translation is due to the fact that bilinguals are less skilled at coping with interference in L2 than in L1, and not to conceptual mediation in one direction rather than the other[79]

Interference in L2 can be noticed in textual translation from Arabic into English, particularly when there is a difference in cultural concepts underlying the lexical items in L1 and L2. The translator in such a case exerts an extra effort to resist the influence of L1 on L2 by trying to find a proper cultural equivalent in L2, which causes a delay in processing. For example, the word da{ *yf* in Arabic means "a visitor to one's home", whether an invited guest or an uninvited one. Underlying this word is the concept of Arab hospitality which is deeply rooted in traditional Arab culture. For ancient Arabs it had been a shame not to show hospitality even to passing travelers with whom one had no previous acquaintance. Hospitality in such a case was even a more celebrated virtue among Arabs than honoring important guests, being related to the Arab value of helping those in trouble. Therefore, in translating (1) from an ancient Arabic text, one translator rendered it as (2).

> (1) Bany 'myr, antum ry'a'un wa d{ayfukum d{ayi'
> (literally: Bani 'myr you are grassroots and your guest is lost),
>
> بني عامر أنتم رعاع وضيفكم ضائع.
>
> (2) *Oh Bani Amer, you are a miserly rabble and your visitors go unattended.*

The translator opted out of the ready equivalent in his bilingual mental lexicon for d{ayf, i.e. the English noun *guest* and chose the generic noun *visitor* to convey the satirical effect intended by the speaker who belongs to a culture which stigmatizes inhospitality to casual visitors and invited guests alike. Thus resisting the *guest* interference, triggered by a superficial interpretation of the Arabic *dayf* and a hasty resort to a mental glossary of literal equivalents, the translator would no doubt require more time and processing to take this lexical decision.

1.3.3.2 Conceptual and lexical transfer: the product

Since languages are different in the way meaning components are combined within concepts and the interrelationships between the lexical entries and the conceptual entries, such differences will be reflected in translation equivalents: "The translator should not expect concepts to be represented the same way in the receptor language as they are in the source language text being translated"[80]

Larson (1997) differentiates between two situations: lexical equivalents when concepts are shared and lexical equivalents when concepts are unknown[81] In the first situation, lexical equivalents could be literal or nonliteral; the nonliteral being the more common between unrelated languages. Nonliteral equivalents come in the form of descriptive phrases and related words. Descriptive phrases are used as equivalents when the source language word is semantically complex and there is no single word in the receptor language that carries the same number of meaning components. For example, there is no single-word equivalent in Arabic for such English nouns as Americanism and Arabism, which mean "an American word/phrase" and "an Arabic word/phrase" respectively. While translating such words from English into Arabic, a translator will have to use a head noun modified by an adjective, e.g. Ta'byr amryki تعبير أمريكي (Literally:an American expression) for the first word and Ta'byr 'rabi تعبير عربي (an Arabic expression) for the second. Related-word equivalents involve synonyms, antonyms, and generic/specific terms in the receptor language. For example, there may be a generic term in the source language for which the receptor language only has a more specific term and vice versa: a specific term in the source language may be translated into a generic term in the receptor language. The latter case is particularly common in the translation of certain abstract nouns from English into Arabic. For example the nouns *resolution* and *decree*, which are hyponyms of the generic term *decision* have only one generic nominal equivalent in Arabic, i.e. *qarar*, which is used in the translation of both these specific terms as well as their generic hypernym *decision*.

In the second situation, i.e. when concepts are unknown in the receptor language, the translator will be overburdened with a dual task of finding an equivalent concept in the receptor culture and a way to express it lexically. Beekman and Callow (1974) list three basic ways in which a translator can find an equivalent expression in the receptor language. These are (1) generic word with a descriptive phrase (2) a loan word (3) a cultural substitute.

A generic term modified with a descriptive phrase can be a translation equivalent when the receptor language has no equivalent for the source language term. For example, in the Hopi language of the USA, *wine* is translated as *fermented grape juice* in the Hopi language. Loan words are words taken from another language and are mostly unknown to the speakers of the receptor language. They include names of people, places, geographical areas, etc. Cultural substitutes represent words for some concepts in the receptor language which are not exactly the same as those for the source language concept. For example, the Armendian word for "coyote" is used as a translation of the English word *wolf* since native speakers of the Armendian language of Mexico do not have the concept Wolf in their surrounding environment[82]

It is worthy of notice that using any one of the formal lexical devices mentioned above in the two cases reviewed by Larson (1997) and Beekman and callow (1974) is a matter of context and register. For example, in translating the English word *wolf* as it occurs in a literary text or a story into the Armendian language of Mexico, the Armendian word for "coyote" may be an acceptable cultural equivalent while in translating a technical document this cultural substitute may not be adequate and a generic term with a modifying phrase is the best lexical equivalent in order to clarify the concept for the receptor language reader.

1.4 Abstract nouns

Abstract nouns, such as *truth* or *beauty*, are defined in the Glossary of Useful Terms as "words that are neither specific nor definite in meaning; they refer to general concepts, qualities, and conditions that summarize an entire category of experience". In the three following sections a review is made of the literature on abstract nouns in the monolingual lexicon, the bilingual lexicon, and finally, in translation from English into Arabic.

1.4.1 Abstract nouns in the monolingual lexicon

Schmid (2000) combines a cognitive paradigm with a broadly functional perspective in a detailed corpus study of 670 so-called shell nouns. The term "shell noun" is coined by the author to refer to the set of abstract nouns as "conceptual shells for complex, proposition-like pieces of information"[83]. Shell nouns fulfill this function by being construed with a "postnominal" clause as in the NP: *the fact that the rest of the world was against him* or by being linked to a complementing clause by means of a copula as in the sentence:*the advantage is that there is a huge audience.* In addition to proposition-like pieces of information, Schmid also looks at shell nouns that have wh-clauses as contents (as in *"I have got to a stage [when I must now look at what is best for my future]"*) as well as infinitives (e.g. A basic rule is [to eat lightly]. With respect to the functions which shell nouns serve, Schmid especially refers to the work by Francis, who has labeled shell nouns as "anaphoric nouns" (1986) and "labels" (1994) which serve to encapsulate stretches of discourse and signal to the reader that more specific information can be found elsewhere in the text[84].

Schmid argues that the images underlying the notions of "encapsulation" and "signaling" motivate his use of the metaphor "shell nouns": shell nouns "supply propositions with conceptual shells which allow speakers to grab them and carry them along as they move on in discourse"; the term shell noun therefore serves a functional purpose since shell nouns "are not defined by inherent properties but constitute a functional linguistic class"[85]

Schmid also examines the relation between shell nouns and the lexicogrammatical patterns they are found in from two sides: he measures the degree to which a certain lexico-grammatical pattern attracts a particular noun (called attraction) and the degree a particular noun relies on a lexico-grammatical pattern for its occurrence (called "reliance")[86]. While the noun *fact*, for instance, turns out to be by far the most frequent noun in the pattern N-CL, its reliance score is significantly lower than that of, for instance, the noun *realization*, because the noun *fact* relies for its use on the pattern N-cl less than does *realization*. Schmid also elaborates on two semantic properties which he considers to be prerequisites for nouns to function as shell nouns, i.e. abstractness and unspecificity"

In her review of Schmid's work, Liesbet (2001) observes that Schmid did not include in his analysis shell nouns which occur in the structure "N+of phrase +ing" as in "the fact of Schmid ignoring this structure"[87]

This typology of abstract nouns as conceptual shells takes into account only the external content these nouns acquire from their syntactical and lexicogrammatical contexts and does not look into the internal conceptual content of abstract nouns which is both inherent and context-free. This will be a major focus in the analysis of abstract nouns in the next chapters. An important assumption related to the study of nouns is that "noun countability is not just an arbitrary grammatical feature of lexical items, but is a very real representation of conceptual content"[88]. It will be my contention in the next chapter that this grammatical feature relates the notions of abstractness and unspecicifity suggested by Schmid to the internal semantic content of abstract nouns, not just to their lexico-grammatical context as shell nouns

1.4.2 Abstract nouns in the bilingual mental lexicon

It is assumed by Kroll (1993) that "translation equivalents for concrete words are likely to share conceptual features, and thus maintain a high degree of semantic overlap[89]. The reason to assume this is that:

> Concrete words refer to entities whose function is likely to be the same across languages. The outward appearance of these entities and the behaviours that they elicit are also likely to be similar across language communities because these relate directly to their functions"[90] (De Groot, 1993).

Abstract words, on the other hand,

> have no external referents that can be looked at, handled, utilized, and thus no guarantee for cross-language similarity in the content of their conceptual representations. Their meanings must be learned by looking their definitions up in a dictionary, having others provide them, or-more

importantly-inferring them from the contexts in which these words are encountered[91].

This conclusion reached by De Groot (1993) was a result of a series of experiments with Dutch-English fluent bilinguals to test the effects of word concreteness and word-frequency on correctness of translations[92]. The wordlists she used included only nouns. This conclusion, however, cannot be taken at face value. For if only concrete words shared conceptual representations across languages, this means that concept mediation would be limited to a restricted class of words. A central claim I will make in the chapters that follow is that some abstract concepts are also shared across languages, something that is reflected in their lexical nominal realizations, which makes them translatable across language pairs.

In actual written translation practice, translation equivalents of abstract nouns will be governed by the same factors outlined in section 1.3.5 either when concepts are shared between the two languages or when they are unknown in the receptor language. An example provided by Larson (1997) is the translation of such English terms as *goodness, holiness, righteousness* and *virtue* into one generic word, *pegkeg* in Aguaruna. A second example is found in translating the English noun *miracle* into an explanatory phrase such as "healing the sick and doing other such deeds" in the Mexican language of Trique since there is no word for *miracle* in this language[93].

1.4.3 Abstract nouns in English-Arabic translation

With regard to the translation of the conceptual content of abstract nouns from English into Arabic, there is no single study dedicated to this subject. Some examples, however, can be found in Baker

(2011) and Anani (1992). Baker (2011) provides the example of the abstract noun *homosexuality* in English, which does not have a ready equivalent in Arabic since" homosexuality" is a culture-specific concept. An explanatory translation such as *shidhwdh jinsi* شـذوذ جنسي (literally: sexual perversion) will just have a pejorative sense and is not acceptable in a neutral context[94] Translation of the English abstract noun *affidavit* is another example given by Baker of unpacking a semantically complex word in English into a superordintate term in Arabic modified by a descriptive phrase. The Arabic equivalent suggested by one translation is: Ifada *Kytabiiya mashfw'a biyamyn* كتابية مشفوعة بيمين إفادة, literally: written communication supported by an oath[95]

Anani (1992) divides translation equivalents of abstract words into two categories. The first of these categories he places under the title 'general abstracta', the second under "modern abstracta"[96] General abstracta are all the Arabic abstract words, be they adjectives, verbs or nouns which have pure Arabic origins and can be translation equivalents to English lexical items. Within this category, Anani (1992) argues, absolute equivalence is almost impossible since the concepts expressed by this type of abstract words are culture-specific and it is this self-same cultural specificity that makes it impossible for the translator to find precise equivalents that carry the same meaning components of the source language word.

Anani gives the example of the word *irony* in English as a literary term. He argues that this word in English has three meaning components which no single Arabic word has: *disparity* (the presence of a situation involving two different situations one of which is unknown to the speaker himself), *sarcasm* (as in "the irony of fate") and *pun* (presence of two meanings, one hidden and an explicit one). Anani concludes that the Arabic word *Sukhriya* سخرية has only the element of sarcasm, since the other two elements are alien to the Arabic culture's usage of the term. Thus he prefers *tawriya sakhyra* تورية ساخرة (literarlly: sarcastic pun) as the accurate translation of the word in its literary sense in drama[97].

It is to be observed that Anani's view of culture is restricted to "cultural heritage" which sees culture as a static and closed system in which meanings of lexical items in the language, which is a subpart of culture, are closely connected to their cultural roots, a belief perhaps encouraged by the lack of updated Arabic dictionaries that record new meanings words acquire through contact with other cultures. From the point of view of the mental lexicon, culture and therefore, language, is a dynamic and changing system in which concepts and words are not tied to their inherent meaning components. It is users, and not cultural constants that add to the meanings of words For example, the Arabic noun *adabiyat* is currently being used as an equivalent of the English noun *literature* (in the sense of 'all the books written on a particular subject'), though its meaning in all classical Arabic dictionaries has to do with literature in the sense of 'literary art'. This proves that languages have common patterns of semantic extension which have nothing to do with their cultural roots. These patterns still need to be investigated carefully. Similarly the Arabic word *Sukhriya* سخرية may acquire the other two meaning components of the English word *irony* through its frequent usage as translation equivalent of this English word.

Thus translation can be an important means of semantic extension in the monolingual mental lexicon. In brief, cultural contact does not only lead to the introduction of new terms into the languages but adds also new meanings to the already existing ones. Second, though absolute equivalence is not possible for all general abstract words, including abstract nouns, there is a broad range of abstract nouns that express language-independent concepts universal to almost all cultures such as the concepts of love, hatred, truth . . . etc. Abstract nouns such as *mathematics, algebra, chemistry* . . . etc have universal meaning components shared by all languages and independent of the their language-specific cultural and derivational origins. The presence of such shared concepts between languages facilitates both conceptual and lexical transfer of these nouns in the translator's mental lexicon and accounts for their translatability, as I will argue more substantively in the next chapters.

The second category of 'modern abstracta' suggested by Anani (1992) includes the words, mostly nouns, that were coined solely for the purpose of translating modern terms in European languages and have no roots in the Arab culture and hence can be considered as complete equivalents to the English words. Words like these include: *Ishtrakiiya* اشتراكية (socialism), *shiyu'iya* شيوعية (communism)[98].

Anani (1992) maintains that there are two factors that influence Arab translators when they translate abstract nouns from English into Arabic. The first of these factors, he argues, is the kind of vocabulary acquisition experiences these translators are put through in their early school years which depend on ready Arabic equivalents the students are provided with in the form of fixed bilingual vocabulary lists. When these students graduate and start to practise translation, these fixed equivalents with fixed meanings still linger on in their memories and affect their lexical choice regardless of the meaning nuances dictated by the context. The second factor is that of mother tongue interference, which Anani finds to be of inescapable influence on the translator's comprehension of the source language (English) and which is a direct consequence of the first factor[99]

Chapter 2

Theories of concepts

2:1 Philosophical roots of the theory of concepts

Of the countless definitions of philosophy, it may be useful for the purposes of our present inquiry to adopt the one provided by Berlin (1979). Philosophy, according to Berlin, is that branch of knowledge which deals with matters lying outside the scope of both formal sciences and empirical sciences. A formal science is a science which discovers new facts through the analysis of already given ones. Examples of formal sciences are mathematics and formal logic. Empirical sciences, on the other hand, are those sciences that try to discover new truths based on methodological observation of phenomena, such as all the natural sciences. A question such as whether time is finite or infinite, for example, cannot be answered either by formal means or empirical methods. So it is a philosophical question. This is why it was not until the forties of the last century, when cognitive psychology established itself as an empirical science, that the study of concepts became independent of the domain of philosophy. However, the study of concepts owes much to the philosophical endeavours of both early philosophers like Aristotle and medieval ones such as St Albertus, St Thomas and Prorphyry. Indeed, all still contribute to present-day discussions in the psychology of concepts and other cognitive sciences.

2:1:1 Concepts in ancient, medieval and modern philosophy

According to Aristotle, there are three acts of reason, which the later medieval logicians called three operations of the mind. The first operation of the intellect, according to Aristotle and St Thomas, concerns conceiving something and grasping its essence without affirming or denying anything about it[100]. Such is the act of knowing through the mental word, which latter-day philosophers call concepts, without saying anything about its existence. Concepts in this first operation cannot be judged to be true or false because a concept is a real "intelligible species" regardless of whether the object it refers to is real or not. For example, though Cinderella does not exist in the real world, a concept of her does exist. The second operation of the mind concerns the relationship between concepts. Concepts are expressed in natural language in the form of statements or "enunciations" which can be judged to be true or false by reference to reality. In this operation, concepts enter into relationships with other concepts through predicating, which is the act of relating a subject to a predicate[101]

The third operation is about using the relationships between statements to form syllogisms[102]. Thus, the first two operations are the ones crucial to us here since they belong to philosophical logic while the third one belongs to formal logic. Aristotle enumerates ten concepts, later called supreme genera, which can be subjects of a predicate. These are: substance, quality, quantity, time, place, action, state, relation, position or affection[103]. Prophyry, another medieval philosopher enumerates five other genera, often called the predicables, which are ways of relating the subject to the predicate. These are: genus, species, property, accident and difference. Genus is the most inclusive of all; it is held to include at least two species as well as their individuals. In his *Metaphysics* Aristotle defines genus with reference to the second operation of the mind as "that which can be predicated of the species and its individuals" and species as 'that which cannot be predicated of the genus'. This means that animal can be a predicate of man, but man cannot be a predicate of animal: we can say man is an animal, but not animal is man.

Porphyry proposes five definitions of difference, the first and most important of which is "that by which species exceeds genus". Aristotle considers difference as the determining factor of the species: "every specific difference united with genus produces species". If we want to translate this definition into present-day language, we can say: every subordinate concept exceeds its superordinate by having more subordinate-specific features added to it while inheriting those of its immediate as well as its remote superordinate. Such is known in modern psychology as the *property inheritance principle* whereby concepts are assumed to be organized in a hierarchical order in such a way that a concept at a lower level inherits the properties of a higher-level concept up to the uppermost superordinate. The inherited properties are then to be added to the lower concept's peculiar features and unique properties. For example, man inherits all the general properties of *animal* and adds to them that of being rational, thus exceeding the genus *animal*.

Property is defined by Aristotle as 'that which does not show what a thing is, but is present to it alone, and reciprocates with the thing'.

Thus, the property of being risible i.e. able to laugh is present in *man* alone but at the same time it does not define the essence of man.

Accident is defined by Aristotle as that which may possibly be present with one and the same thing and may not be present. Prophyry offers other two definitions of accident as "that which is present and absent without the destruction of its subject and also as "that which is neither genus, nor difference, nor species, nor property, yet is always inherent in a subject". Being tall is an example of accident with regard to man. Thus the difference between accident and property is that property is present to one species alone while accident is not species-specific.

In my opinion, the difference between property and accident is that while both are inherent in a subject, the inherency of accident is perceived by the intellect when accident moves from potency to actuality while the inherency of property is always salient to the mind whether or not it is moved from potency to actuality. Thus accident is contingently connected to the species. This means that it is inherent in the individuals, yet this inherency is recognized only when it appears in them. Property, on the other hand, is necessarily connected to the species, that is, recognizably inherent in it whether it appears in the individuals or not.

In post-Renaissance philosophy, cognition becomes central to the study of concepts. In the first sentence of the Introduction of "a Critique of pure reason", Kant claims "that all our knowledge begins with experience there can be no doubt." He goes on to say, "but, though all our knowledge begins with experience, it by no means follows that all arises out of experience. For, on the contrary, it is quite possible that our empirical knowledge is a compound of that which we receive through impressions, and that which the faculty of cognition supplies from itself."[104] Kant came to believe that a knowledge existed which was altogether independent of experience, and even of all sensuous impressions; he called it *a priori* knowledge. This knowledge we ourselves contribute to the world. For example, ideas of absolute space and absolute time did not arrive through our senses.

Kant's ideas in this regard came as a reaction to the English philosopher john lock's empirical philosophy in the late seventeenth century[105]. Lock thought that the concept of space is acquired by the infant through observation. By watching the movement of objects, it gradually infers or learns this concept. The same applies to time. Lock argued that we learn the concept of time by observing that events occur in a temporal sequence. Kant found these two arguments to be illogical. The concept of object, Kant argues, presupposes the concept of space since an object is something which takes up some space and it is impossible to conceive the existence of an object with no length or breadth or width. Similarly for time, any sequence of events perceived by the mind presupposes the concept of time, for without this concept preexisting, this sequence of events could not be perceived in the first place. Kant concludes, then, that space and time must be a priori properties of the mind or perception and not of the world.

The sense impressions received are manipulated, categorized and eventually presented to ourselves within the bounds of these great intrinsic concepts, i.e. we fit things within our awareness of space and time. From this manipulation of sensory data within our intrinsic a priori knowledge arise our basic concepts/ideas[106]

2:1:2 A logical account of concepts

We can argue that language forms the base of a triangle whose two sides are logic and psychology. The hierarchy of concepts in our minds can be expressed in logical statements composed of subject and predicate. The only vehicle of this expression is language. Let us probe the issue.

2:1:2:1 Intension and extension of concepts

It has just been pointed out that *difference* is defined as that by which the species exceeds the genus. It follows from the definition that there must inevitably be a set of elements comprehended in the genus which the species exceeds by another set comprehended in that species alone and added to whatever the species inherits from the genus. Whatever is comprehended in the genus and the species as such is a set of defining attributes whereby their applicability to particular individuals is determined. Such is what is known in the Port Royal logic as *comprehension* and in modern schools of logic as *intension*[107]

In his *Metaphysics*, Aristotle links comprehension to both species and genus when he says" species partake of genera, but not genera of species, since the species accepts the definition of genus, but not genus that of the species". For example, *man* accepts the definition of *animal* and overspecifies it by man-specific features, but animal does not accept the definition of man.

An intensional definition is defined by De saussaire (1916) and Palmer (1999) as "the necessary and sufficient conditions" for belonging to the set being defined. By necessary is meant that the parts of the definition must be in the entity or else it is not a member of the set being defined. For example, if man is defined as a rational animal, this means that rationality and animateness are two intensional properties that must be present in a thing in order for that thing to belong to the set of all men. By sufficient is meant that a thing that has all the intensional properties mentioned in the definition must belong to the set being defined, regardless of the other properties it has. In our present example, it is sufficient for a thing to be rational and animate in order to belong to the set "man", regardless of the other properties it may have such as being emotional, for example.

Intension, then, represents a relationship of many to one, that is a relationship between the species, their individuals and the genus since 'all partake of the genus'. The inverse relationship is that obtaining between the genus and its consequent species and individuals; it is a relationship of one to many since all are contained under the genus. This relationship is known as *extension*. Etymologically, extension is derived from the Latin word *extensio*, which literally means a *"stretch."* The very notion of extension implies a relation of one to many, or a stretching out (extension) of one to embrace the many"[108]. In this way, extension is related to both genus and species. Extension of a concept 'consists of all the things to which the concept applies'[1]. Thus, extension of man is the set of all men who ever existed in the present or the past or will exist in the future.

---

[1]   Note on terminology: the term *extension* is used in two senses .The first sense is that of the whole set of objects to which a concept applies. The second, which is the more dominant in this book, is that of an individual member of this set. This usage is based on Frisch (1979).Frisch (1979) uses the term *intension* to mean either (A) the definition of a concept or (B) an instance of this definition. By analogy, I use the term *extension* in these two ways, either to refer to a whole set or just a single member

It is assumed in logic that the greater the intension of a concept, the lesser its extension. This assumption is known as *the law of inverse ratio*[109]. This law is in keeping with the property inheritance principle since the more we go down from the genera to the species, properties of the immediate and superordinate genera are inherited by the consequent species and added to those already present in their intensions. At the same time, the number of individuals to which the concept applies decreases as we go more and more specific. So the extension of mammal is narrower than that of animal, and the extension of man is narrower than that of mammal and so on.

2:1:2:2 The common ground between logic and psychology

Aristotle and the medieval philosophers established a line of demarcation between logic and psychology by differentiating between the first operation of the mind and the second and third operations of the mind. Logic is concerned with the relationship between concepts as a basis of reasoning and forming syllogisms, considering them in as much as they are bound in words. Psychology, on the other hand, is concerned with the concept as a cognitive phenomenon independently of any relationship with words. Psychology in this sense is a branch of knowledge which is concerned with the relationship between concepts and things, be they real entities or imagined ones. One can argue that language is a common factor between psychology and logic. On the one hand, a point of conversion between psychology and language is found in the area of meaning since meaning is represented mentally as a set of semantic features. On the other hand, language is the vehicle whereby logic transforms internal or implicit relations between concepts into explicit relations expressed in statements composed of subject and predicate.

2:2 Psychological theories of concepts

In this section, three major views of concepts are presented. Later, we integrate the three into one theoretical and methodological framework that suits the purposes of our subsequent study of abstract nouns in the bilingual lexicon.

2:2:1 The classical view of concepts

All that we have discussed so far leads us to our present discussion of the classical view of concepts. This view, which dates back to Aristotle, hinges on three basic assumptions. Firstly, concepts are represented by a set of necessary and sufficient features. Secondly, each representation is a summary description of an entire class. Thirdly, features of superordinate concepts are nested (included) in the subordinates[110]

The first of these assumptions constitutes the core of the classical view. A necessary feature is one that must be present in every instance (extension) of the concept. Once a set of features characteristic of a given concept are present in an instance, it must belong under this concept. As such these features are said to be jointly sufficient to define the concept. Necessary and sufficient features of a concept are also called *defining features*.

The second assumption refers to the fact that concepts do not represent instances or exemplars but a whole class of objects. This means that a concept is the ultimate product of a process of abstraction from particular instances experienced by the senses through the reasoning faculty of the mind. Being a summary description of an entire class of entities, the representation of a concept has fewer features than the representation of each individual instance to which the concept applies. Thus, a major constraint placed on the features used in this summary representation is that they must be general, that is, a single feature should be capable of being used to characterize many concepts in a domain[111].

The features included in a summary representation are of two types. There are perceptual features and abstract features. Perceptual features are outputs of the human perceptual system. They include such features as those related to curvatures in the representation of a geographical concept such as *mountain* or body proportions or height in the representation of the concept *boy*. Abstract features are those features that cannot be perceived sensually but are instantiated by perceptual features. For example, the abstract features *male+*, *human+* and *young+* are instantiated by the perceptual features of height and hairstyle. The relationship between abstract features and perceptual features is a reciprocal one. Whereas perceptual features instantiate abstract features, the latter can dictate the former's nature. For example, the abstract features *human*, male and *young* necessitate other concrete features related to the hormone activity, such as body proportions. For object concepts, the abstract features could be functional ones. For example, the functional feature "used for transportation" can be considered as an abstract feature of the concept *vehicle*[112].

A related distinction in this regard is made between *the concept core* and *the identification procedure*. A concept core may include perceptual features and/or abstract features. For example, the representation of the concept *chair* can include the perceptual feature "have a seat and the abstract one "used for seating". An identification procedure contains only perceptual features such as those of size, height . . . etc. The major function of the concept core is to relate a concept to other concepts. For example, the abstract feature *human* relates the concept *boy* to the concept *man*. Perceptual features in an identification procedure are used in making category decisions about concepts. When the concept core includes mainly perceptual features, there is no need to resort to the identification procedure for categorization. For instance, the core feature *have four angles* is sufficient for categorizing an item as a square. The concept core is used mainly in semantic tasks while identification procedures are used mostly in perceptual tasks[113].

The last of the three basic assumptions of the classical view is *the nesting assumption*[114]. According to this assumption, if concept *X* is a subset of concept *Y*, then the defining features of y are nested in those of x. So if *ostrich* is a subset of *bird*, it follows that the defining features of bird are included in *ostrich*. At the same time ostrich has its own defining features which distinguish it from other birds. These same defining features of ostriches will be nested in their subspecies which in turn will have their own defining features that distinguish them from each other and so on. In a hierarchy, this is also called the *property inheritance principle*, to which we have often referred. Another principle which follows from this assumption is known as the *transitivity principle*. It can be expressed as follows: suppose that there are three concepts X, Y and Z. Given that Y is a subset of X and Z is a subset of Y, it must follow that Z is a subset of X. Thus the relationship between X, Y and Z is a transitive relationship. If we say that a bird is an animal and a robin is a kind of bird, then a robin is an animal too. Fig (1) rpresents the transitive relationship holding between concepts and their subordinates in a hierarchy[115].

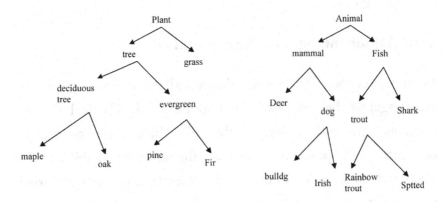

The hierarchy tree of Fig (1) represents the transitivity of IS-A links between concepts but not the transitivity of their properties. For example, perhaps linked to evergreens is the property "has needles", and linked to oak is the property "has lobed leaves". Semantic networks can represent all transitivity relations based on the inheritance principle, as Fig (2) shows.

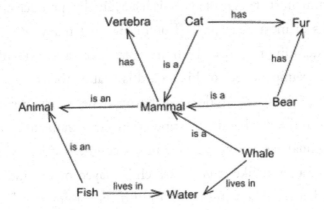

Fig 2: An example of a semantic network

Since the 1970s, several empirical and theoretical criticisms have been directed at the classical view. In the following section, I review these criticisms with respect to the three basic assumptions discussed above.

2:2:2 Arguments against the classical view

In this subsection, we discuss the theoretical and empirical arguments raised against the three basic assumptions of the classical view of concepts. This will be done in the order these assumptions were presented in the previous subsection. The aim is to rehabilitate the classical view in order to use it subsequently, together with other views about concepts, in constructing a definitional theory for abstract concepts that we can use in a decompositional analysis of abstract nouns either as independent lexical items or in the process of lexical transfer in the translator's bilingual mind.

2:2:2:1 Arguments against the first assumption

A basic criticism leveled at the first assumption of the classical view is the argument that years of analysis have failed to produce clear-cut definitions of most concepts[116] This means that many concepts do not have defining features which are both necessary and sufficient. A famous example cited in this regard is that of the concept *game*. This concept, it is argued, does not have any necessary or sufficient features. On the one hand, any stipulation that a game must involve two individuals as a necessary feature is counter-evidenced by the presence of a game like *solitaire*, which is played by one individual. On the other hand, a feature like "must divert or entertain" is not a sufficient one since it is present in many things other than games, whistling, for instance[117]. Another example provided by Murphy

(2004). is that of the planet Pluto. Astronomers in 2000 have rightly questioned its planethood, but there is nothing to do about it now after decades of its discovery. This means that the definition of the concept planet is not sufficient to include all the items that are designated by the name of the concept.

Murphy (2004) argues that concepts cannot be equated with definitions since the properties listed by subjects in empirical tests for different concepts are not defining. He cannot find a single necessary feature for defining the concept *dog*, for example. Barking cannot be considered, he maintains, a necessary feature since there are dogs which, due to some accident, cannot bark.

2:2:2:2 Arguments against the second assumption

The second criticism is related to the view of a concept as a summary representation of an entire class. It is argued that this assumption focuses only on the perceptual or structural features of concepts to the exclusion of more abstract or functional features. For example, the representation of the concept *cup* within the classical view, according to this criticism, will encompass dimensional features like shape and concavity while the core defining feature of *cup* might be the functional, more abstract one "used for drinking liquids". This argument was put forth by Nelson (1974) and Anglin (1977) and is motivated by the fact that most of the perceptual tasks related to category membership use only visual stimuli and therefore focus mainly on concrete features.

2:2:2:3 Arguments against the third assumption

The third and by far the most pervasive criticism leveled against the classical view is related to the nesting of features. It is assumed that due to this principle, the classical view fails to explain three important phenomena in the psychology of concepts: prototypicality, cases of intransitivity in a hierarchy and the presence of borderline cases. In what follows, each of these three phenomena is examined in order to show how, according to these criticisms, the classical view fails to account for each of them separately.

2:2:2:3:1 Prototypicality in the classical view

Prototypicality is the extent to which a category member is representative of the whole category. This prototypicality is measured by having subjects rate how typical an item is as a category member. Items with the highest scores are considered the most typical within a category and those with the lowest scores are considered the least typical. For example, Smith and Medin (1981) concluded from typicality ratings that robin and sparrow are considered typical birds, hawk and eagle less typical and chicken and penguin atypical. It was also found that prototypicality affects people's efficiency in categorization. There are tests in which subjects are presented with category names and category members and nonmembers. The category in such tests is called *the target* and the item is called *probe*. Subjects are asked to decide whether each probe is a member or nonmember of the target concept. It was found that subjects are slower at making correct decisions for atypical than for typical items[118]. For example, when *bird* is the target concept, test items corresponding to robin and sparrow were categorized more quickly than those corresponding to eagle and hawk, which in turn were categorized faster than chicken and goose. The basic determinant of typicality in such tests is family resemblance, which means that typicality of an item is determined by the features it has which are shared by other members of the same category[119]. Family resemblance is calculated in two steps. First, each feature listed for a subset is weighted by the total number of subsets it is listed for. Then, the weights of all its features are summed. The subset with the highest result is considered the most typical. Thus *chair* was calculated to be the most typical furniture because it was found to share more features with other furniture items than any of these items does.

Critics of the classical view argue that this view has nothing to say about the typicality of concepts[120]. Since the defining features of concept X are equally nested in its subordinates, then there is no difference between them in so far as they are representations of the superordinate category, which contradicts the prototypicality effects we have outlined above. Thus, typical and atypical members within the classical view will equally be good members of the category. Typicality variations, accordingly, must be accounted for in terms of variations in subordinate-specific, nondefining features, something which the classical view prohibits.

2:2:2:3:2 Cases of intransitivity

Hampton (1982) has shown that people do not always follow the rules of transitivity that are found in a strict hierarchy. For example, his subjects verified that a car seat was an example of chair. They also agreed that chair is an example of furniture. But they denied that a car seat was a kind of furniture. If people were tracing the links in the IS-A hierarchy, they would not have denied this relation, since subjects did agree that each individual link was correct. Another example provided by Hampton is that of the concept CLOCK. While his subjects decided that a clock is an item of furniture and that Big Bin is a clock, they still denied that Big Bin is furniture[121].

2:2:2:3:2 Borderline cases

The third criticism related to the nesting assumption concerns the presence of unclear cases that stand on a borderline between two concepts. According to this criticism, if properties of a superordinate concept are nested in its subordinates, there should be no problem in deciding that a concept X is a subset of concept Y since one will have to just compare defining features to reach a decision thereof. Besides, people disagree as to categorizing one item as a member of a given category. Even the same person may change his mind about a subset relation on different occasions. In one experiment conducted by McCloskey and Cluckseberg (1978), their subjects changed their minds about 22 % of the time about such cases as whether an olive is a fruit or vegetable. Of eight categories investigated by Hampton (1979), seven categories formed a continuum with no clear-cut boundaries in between. His subjects barely included sinks as members of the kitchen utensils category.

2:2:3 Other views of concepts

There are other two views besides the classical view which try to overcome the latter's shortcomings. The first one is known as the probabilistic view. This view combines both necessary and non-necessary features in its representation of concepts and assigns each feature a weight according to its likelihood of occurrence with a concept or a concept member. For example, in the representation of the concept *bird*, a probabilistic model would list such necessary features as "winged" and "feathered" along with such non-necessary ones as "flies" and "sings" but it would assign the latter lower rates than the former, since they are unlikely to occur with such bird members as chicken and duck.

Typicality is explained by the probabilistic view in the same manner. For example, people rate robin as more typical as a bird than chicken because the non-necessary features *flies* and *sings* are assigned as equally high weight for robin as the necessary ones of *feathered* and *winged*, while for chicken only the necessary features are given any weight at all. Thus, the probabilistic view converges with the classical view on the assumption that a concept is a summary representation of a whole class in the form of a set of features and diverges with it on the latter's assumption that only necessary features should be included in the representation.

The second view is known as the exemplar view. This view holds that concepts are represented by their exemplars. On the surface, this view seems to contradict the other two views which assume that a concept is a summary representation of an entire class rather than a single instance. Besides, it seems counter-intuitive since a concept by definition is an abstraction based on an indefinite number of exemplars. However, the contradiction disappears as soon as we know that the word *exemplar* is used in two senses, either as a single example of a concept or a subset of that concept. An exemplar of the concept *clothing* could either be "my faded blue jeans" or the subset of all blue jeans. Hence, even the exemplar view permits abstractions[122]. If the exemplar is an instance, it must be represented as a set of properties. If it is a subset, its representation could be other exemplars or a description of the relevant properties.

2:2:4 Re-establishing the classical view

There have been many efforts to salvage the classical view against the criticisms leveled at it. I will review some of these attempts and deploy other arguments in defence of the classical view against the three critical arguments mentioned above.

2:2:4:2 Summary representation counterargument

The second argument put forth against the classical view by Nelson (1974) and Anglin (1977), who insist that the classical view prohibits abstract, functional features from a summary representation, is held by Smith & Medin (1981) to be based on a false premise[123]. They argue that there is nothing in the classical view's summary representation which excludes functional features from a summary representation. A functional feature, such as the fact that a cup can hold liquid, can be used in a summary description of an entire class, can be singly necessary and be part of a jointly sufficient set and can be nested in other feature sets.

Indeed the generality constraint required of a summary representation of a concept necessitates the incorporation of abstract features into this representation. Abstract features have far wider applicability than perceptual ones and will help us economize on the features needed in the representation. Miller &Johnson-Laird (1976) proved that perceptual features are by no means adequate to cover all the items belonging to a conceptual domain. One of the illustrative examples they provide is that of the concept *table*. They list for *table* three perceptual features "1 connected and rigid, 2) has a flat and horizontal top. 3) has vertical legs. Some of these features, according to Miller and Johnson-Laird, are not true of all tables. For instance, many drafting tables do not have a horizontal top. If we replace the feature "has a flat and horizontal top" with the functional feature "has a top capable of support", drafting tables can easily be included in the general concept of tables.

2:2:4:3 A case for prototypicality and borderline cases

There are some attempts to account for typicality and borderline cases within the classical view. These attempts are in the form of theoretical arguments challenging the basic arguments put forward against the classical view.

2:2:4:3:1 Prototypicality counterargument

According to Smith&Medin (1981), there is nothing in the classical view which prohibits non-defining subordinate-specific features from accounting for typicality effects. This can be proven by adding a hypothetical, defining F0 feature to, say, all furniture items. This feature adds a constant of six to the sum weights of each item, which increases its score by the value of this constant. For example, suppose that 5, 6, 4, 5, 3, 2, are the weights of the features F1, F2, F3, F4, F5, F6 listed for *chair*. The addition of the defining feature F0 to all the six furniture items adds a weight to the score of each item equally. This means that the defining features do not affect the consistency of typicality scores which are based on non-defining ones.

2:2:4:3:3 The borderline counterargument

In answering the border-line criticisms outlined in 2.2.2.3, Smith& Medin (1981) argue that the nesting assumption does not guarantee that decisions about subset relations should be clear-cut, leaving no room for unclear cases. They mention two reasons in support of this argument. First, many of the concepts we carry around in our heads are not complete due to some missing defining features. This will make us uncertain about whether a tomato is a fruit or vegetable, for instance. Second, a concept may have two definitions, a common definition and a technical one. Technically, a tomato can be judged to be a kind of fruit (it has seeds), but considering its everyday usage as a food ingredient (in salads, for example), we may judge it to be a vegetable.

Chapter 3

The Classical View Revisited

3:1 A cognitive rehabilitation of the classical view

In this subsection I make a theoretical as well as an empirical endeavour to rehabilitate the classical view of concepts on a cognitive as well as a cognitive-semantic foundation and reconcile it with the exemplar and probabilistic theories in a new, hybridized theoretical framework. This rehabilitation is focused on three major aspects:the classical view's defining features, the summary representation principle and the cases of intransitivity, borderline cases and prototypicality issues.

3:1:1 The classical view's defining features

The first critical argument, the one directed at the classical view's "defining features", can be split into three subarguments each of which will be critically analyzed. The first subargument says that the classical view is a fiasco since no necessary and sufficient features could be detected for 'most concepts'. This means that concepts are of two types: strict concepts for which there are necessary and sufficient features and other fuzzy ones for which there are no straight features which are both necessary and sufficient. The latter type, according to this subargument, represents the majority of concepts. This means that concepts are not inherently fuzzy because if they were, no concept whatsoever could have clear-cut defining features. What is it then that makes for the fuzziness or the clearcutness of concepts?

One possible answer is our degree of knowledge of the natural world and how far the artificial world has developed. The first part of this answer relates to concepts of natural objects while the second part relates to those of man-made objects. Before planets were discovered, no clear-cut definition of the concept *planet* was ready at hand. That Pluto has passed for a planet for hundreds of years while only recently it has been discovered to violate the supposedly necessary features of planets does not refer to any fuzziness in the concept, but rather in this particular instance. Furthermore, the fact that its planethood has withstood the drag of time for all these decades attests to a faculty in the human mind which approximates instances to the nearest category.

As for concepts of man-made objects, let us illustrate by giving the example of the concept *telephone*. The word *telephone* was coined in 1840. At that time the concept was only related to the Greek origin of the word which simply meant "distant voice" or "transmission of voice over distance". When the telephone was invented and the first public telephone service introduced in the 1870s, no particular purpose could yet be envisaged for the device. On March 1877, the New York daily telegraphic carried a front-page headline warning against the 'terrors of the telephone'. The daily telegraphic article held the telephone to pose a danger to the press as a public address system. This was because the use of the telephone as a dialogic rather than a monologic device was not yet established[124]

Later on, when the concept was settled as telephones became widespread as devices for interpersonal communication the features *dialogic* and *long distance* became necessary and sufficient features of the concept *telephone*. Now these two features are necessary but not sufficient features in the definition of the concept *telephone* since computers can do the job equally well. However, there is no intrinsic technological barrier which precludes the invention, at any future time, of a digital phone-shaped device which can be attached to any computer or laptop to do the function of the old analogue telephone yet at a cheaper rate and still bear the name *telephone*. There is no intrinsic social or technological barrier too that this device will replace the analogue phone and the digital PC in dialogic communication. When this happens the concept *telephone* will have recovered its necessary and sufficient features as a dialogic device for interpersonal long-distance communication. Thus a concept can develop from having no defining features at all to having strict classical-view defining features and then relapse into being a fuzzy concept before it re-settles into a supposedly final state. The message is that the presence of necessary and sufficient features is not a pre-given fact but is relative to the degree to which the world of man-made objects has evolved and how far our knowledge has kept pace with this evolution.

By necessary features, then, we should be meaning cognitive necessity rather than logical necessity. There is no part in the classical view which insists we should not.

The second subargument of the first critical argument challenges the assumption that our definition of an object represents our concept of it. We can argue that concepts represent our implicit knowledge about things while definitions represent explicit knowledge of them. This explicit knowledge is constructed by sophisticated semanticists and will be exact according as our knowledge of the world is complete and relative to how far the world has changed. Definitions, then, are just reflections of the cognitive world and the real world and if they are inadequate, this is because the worlds they represent are.

There is an element of modality, usually lost on the critics, in the classical view's assumption about defining features. The classical view does not actually say that definitions *are* composed of defining features, but simply that for features to be defining they *have to* be necessary and sufficient. The fact that there are many concepts in the world which do not conform to this model is not the fault of the classical view but rather a defect in the world and in our conceptual structure.

In other words, the classical view is not a cognitive theory of concepts; indeed it is a metacognitive one. Metacognition is defined as "cognition about cognition", or "knowing about knowing.[125]. It refers to one's knowledge concerning one's own cognitive processes or anything related to them. Folk metacognition is an evaluative judgment about one's knowledge, like when an eye witness asserts before a judge that his memory never fails him regarding the events he witnesses. The classical view turns this evaluative metacognition into a formalized modal one. It provides a model for the way definitions have to be, not what they really are, ipso facto, in our cognitive world. If our cognitive knowledge of a given object is not complete, our metacognitive knowledge of this cognitive knowledge will be incomplete too. Our knowledge is psychologically represented by our cognition while 'our knowledge of our knowledge' is discursively represented by our metacognition. The classical view is about the latter, not the former. Nevertheless, in the last section of our critical review of the different criticisms against the classical view, we will see that even our metacognitive knowledge can be complete in the absence of perfect cognitive knowledge if we possess the necessary tools to analyze our intuitions. This will certainly overhaul our cognitive gaps and is an achievement the classical view has to its credit.

Now let us turn to the third subargument of the first argument raised against the classical view, which maintains that the classical view's necessary features must be present in all category members all the time; otherwise the classical view runs into serious trouble. So if, for example, one should run against a dog which, due to some accident, had lost its bark, this means that the definition of a dog as "a mammal which has a barking sound", is not an ironclad definition of a dog. The problem with this view is that it interprets the classical view's 'category member' rather too literally as a physical instance or exemplar in the real world rather than as an abstraction in the world of mind. The single instance of the dog which lost its bark maps to a subset of animals in our minds whose other members we have seen before barking. This physical dog is a real-world extension of the concept *dog* while the subset of dogs in the inner world of cognition is a conceptual extension of this concept. The exemplar in which the dog-properties are present is the subset *dog*, in an exemplar view sense, not the faulty physical instance in the real world. If the exemplar view has an interpretation for the exemplar as an abstraction which represents an entire subset, such an interpretation is more worthy of the classical view which has far wider room for abstraction than the other two views. Indeed the classical view converges with the exemplar view on this aspect.

3:1:2 The classical view's summary representation

It is obvious, then, that abstract features satisfy the requirements of a summary representation more than perceptual ones do and that they are to be sought in the concept core rather than in the identification procedure[2]. We assume, for this reason, that abstract features are also the ones involved in the summary representations of conceptual combinations. Let us verify this assumption.

3:1:2:1 Abstract features in conceptual combinations

Since concept cores rather than identification procedures are used in relating a concept to other concepts, they are likely to be the ones involved in conceptual combinations. One can argue that conceptual combinations are just the product of the interplay between an overspecifying concept and the abstract core of an overspecified concept. If concept A combines with concept B to form concept C, the resulting C is a conceptual combination of A and B. In this case A represents an overspecification of B. The overspecification could be either analytic or synthetic. An analytic overspecifying concept is an internal recursive feature of the concept which is identified by semantic analysis. A synthetic overspecifying concept represents an external feature whereby the concept as a whole is restricted through

---

2   Note on terminology: the adjective *abstract* is used in two senses. Sometimes it is used to mean "general", that is, forming a generalization or an abstraction as in the phrase *abstract sets*. The other, more common sense is that of "non-concrete". . But it is crucial here to stress that I use the term *abstraction* when I refer nominally to the first sense and abstractness when referring to the second sense.

conceptual synthesis. For example, when the concept *police* combines with the concept *car,* the result is the concept *police car.* The concept *police* introduces an external overpecification of the core feature "used for transportation" of the concept *car* without interfering with the latter's perceptual features. The overspecifying concept as such introduces an implicit or an explicit perceptual element to the concept it combines with which does not intersect with the identification procedure of that concept.

Other examples that illustrate what I mean by synthetic combination are those formed in combination with the concept *chair,* e.g. swivel chair, rocking chair, folding chair, wherein the overspecifying concepts *swivel, rocking* and *folding* are externally related to the functional core "used for seating" in a general way rather than to a specific seating function for which a chair is used. Nor do they relate to specific identification features like "having a seat" "having legs" since any chair whatsoever can be fitted with rockers, can be designed so as to be folded, to swivel . . . etc without this being tied to any specific function or a basic perceptual feature of *chair.* Conceptual combinations formed in this way will be called **types**. That is, they are types of the overspecified concept *chair.*

Now let's consider other chair exemplars: Car seat, garden chair, barber chair. In addition to reflecting the functional seating core, these chair exemplars are closely related to a perceptually observable recursive variable, that of "the specific place in which the chair is used". We detect this recursive variable through a method of statistical semantic analysis of lexical items that is explained in detail below. Unlike types, such conceptual combinations are formed analytically by filling in an internal variable in the identification procedure of the concept itself so that it restricts the concept's abstract core in a specific way. The internality and specificity of this variable are verified by empirical and theoretical methods that are discussed in detail in the present section. I will call conceptual combinations formed by analysis conceptual extensions of a concept. I will also call the internal variable which combines analytically with the concept core in a specific way to form an extension the **central identification criterion** (CIC).

The central identification criterion for a given concept can be discovered by close semantic analysis of a considerable number of items pertaining to this concept. We can define the central identification criterion as that by which perceptual features are combined with the concept core to form a conceptual extension. Table (1) illustrates some object concepts from different domains together with their perceptual features, abstract features and the conceptual types and extensions related to each. The analysis of the data supplied by the table shows that the abstract functional features forming the concept cores are the axis around which both the identification procedure and the central identification criterion revolve.

Table (1): The central identification criterion.

Types	Extensions	Identification criterion	Abstract features (Concept core)	Perceptual features	Generic equivalent	Concept Name
Rocking chair Swivel chair Folding chair	Garden chair Barber chair Car seat	Specific place	Used for sitting on	Having a seat Four legs	Seat	Chair
Race car Motor car Police car Patrol car	Truck Bus Pickup Private car Freight car Passenger car Van	Type of Load	Used for transportation	Four-wheels motor	Automobile machine	Car
Frying pan Roaster Drip pan	Omelette pan Patty pan	Food	Used for cooking	Metal vessel		Pan
Console table Drop-leaf table Pedestal table Trestle table worktable	Kitchen table Dressing table Card table Operating table Conference table Communication table counter	Place	Used for placing things on	Legs Supported board		Table
Carpet bag Overnight bag Gripsack Handbag Evening bag Shoulder bag Clutch bag Plastic bag Sleeping bag Sandbag Sweatbag Icebag Teabag Beanbag Bladder Golfbag Backpack Burlap bag Drawstring bag carryall	Garment bag Weekender Luggage Etui Ragbag Purse Carrier bag Schoolbag Sickbag Skin Tucker-bag Toolbag Spongebag Toiletbag postbag bookbag shopping bag dustbag game bag burnbag	Contents	Used For Carrying things around.			Bag

3:1:2:1:1 A baseline of psychological analysis

All the concepts exemplified in table (1) are concepts of man-made objects. Since human beings are motivated in their manufacture of things by a given purposeful need for the thing manufactured, so abstract functional features are expected to be more easily recognizable in concepts of man-made objects than in those of the natural world. The items analysed represent concepts at the middle level of categorization, which is also called the *generic level of categorization* and *the basic level of categorization*[3]. It is widely believed that this level is the best level for categorizing objects and by far the most widely used in everyday communication. This belief is consistent with studies made by Callanan (1985), which assert the fact that basic category names are more frequently used than superordinate and subordinate names, and those made by Corter and Gluck (1992). Corter and Gluck (1992) developed a metric that they called category utility and proved that it can correctly predict the preferred level of categorization by measuring reaction time in naming experiments. Their results are consistent with psychological explanations for the advantages of the generic level.

This level is also preferred here for producing a classical view model of concepts since items belonging under a middle-level category are

---

[3]   Note on terminology: the adjective *generic* is used in two senses: a technical sense and a non-technical one. The technical sense is the one which we encounter in the literature on the psychology of concepts. In this sense, generic level, for example, refers to the middle level of categorization. . The non-technical sense is "general" i.e related to the genus rather than the species. An example of this usage is the phrase *generic name*. The noun *Animal* is the generic name of the concept animal in contrast to beast, which is a generic equivalent, that is, equivalent of this general name.

more similar and featurally symmetrical than those at a superordinate level. At the same time, they are more distinctive than items at a subordinate level, which are indistinguishable from each other to a non-expert eye. An identification criterion, then, is more likely to be detected for category items at the middle level.

3:1:2:1:2 Logical analysis

We can look at the relationship between extensions of a generic-level concept and their central identification criterion as a function which attributes a specific value to each argument x in its domain. The range of values of x in the case of *chair* is places which chairs are designed for. Each extension is an argument in the domain of f and each argument is assigned a place-value, as can be seen in table (2).

Table 2: examples of functions

Generic concept	Function f	Domain	Range
Chair	Place for x	Chairs	Specific places
Bag	Content of x	Bags	Personal items
Table	Place of x	Tables	Specific places
Pan	Content of x	Pans	Particular foods
Vehicle	Load of x	Vehicles	Particular loads
Knife	Cutting object of x	Knives	Cutting objects

Whenever a central identification criterion is detected, it brings us closer to a classical view definition of a concept at the generic level and its abstract exemplars (extensions) at specific levels. At a generic level the CIC represents a function f as can be seen in table 2. Place of x, for example is a function which accepts chairs as its arguments and attributes to them as their values *specific places which they are designed for.* In this way, each conceptual extension x is assigned a value in R, the range of values of f whereby this extension is identified as a member of the category. A concept at the generic level can be defined only in terms of *f.* This can be done by applying *f* to all arguments of the domain. The result will be all the values in R attached to the concept. Since this will make a complex definition, we can instead resort to f as an abstract function, to the exclusion of its domain and range. Thus we can define a chair as a *piece of furniture which is made for seating one person in a given place*[4]. Each chair extension will be defined by replacing the identification variable *a given place* with a place-value, i.e. an item of R.Concepts and their extensions having thus been defined, there remain the types. Each type is defined by adding its overspecifying concept to the definition of the generic concept. An armchair can be defined as a piece of furniture with an arm, made for the seating of one person. It is important to notice here that a type has potentially wider applicability than the extension and the concept name because it is not constrained by a central identification criterion and therefore is not assigned a central identification value. So a *bell chair* can be any chair and can be made for use anywhere.

A type is related to the concept as a whole and not to its central identification criterion. So a swivel chair can, in principle at least,

---

[4] Clearly this is a nominalist definition since it excludes the types considering them just as nominal overspecifications of a concept, which is only a name in itself. If we apply extra-lexical knowledge we may find that the types of chair are in fact extensions, since each type is almost restricted to a place value or a few values in R. For example rocking chair is mostly found in gardens. A swivel chair can be found either in an office or a barber's shop but not in a car, for instance. However it is an intermediary step towards a logical definition which keeps extensions and types differentiated semantically both as conceptual entities and real-world entities.

be found anywhere. In more precise terms, it does not pick an item-value from R but relates to f as a whole. In this respect it is on the same generic plane as the concept to which it is related; it is simply the concept restricted by an external overspecifying element. The overspecifying feature of a given type, being arbitrarily combined with a concept, cannot be predicted and therefore cannot be specified as a finite taxonomic set or sets; many types can be formed by a free combination of concepts. On the contrary, the overspecifying feature of an extension can be considered as part of a finite set of elements constrained by a central identification criterion. We will call the external overspecifying concept of a given type the **peripheral identification criterion (PIC).**

The diversity with which external, overspecifying features can combine with concepts to form different types becomes clear when we analyze the 68 chair items found in Wordnet English Dictionary. The analysis reveals that the peripheral overspecification criteria introduced by the external concepts fall into five categories: shape (e.g: bell chair, balloon chair, ladder-back chair), function (e.g: reclining chair, feeding chair, ducking stool), movement (rocking chair, swivel chair, stroller), added part (armchair, wheelchair, side chair), spatial dimension (chaise long, taboret), quality (easy chair, overstuffed chair). Except for the functional category, as the analysis will show, the overspecifying features in all chair types belonging under the other four categories do not affect the basic perceptual features of *chair*, i.e. those of having a seat supported on the ground and a back. From now onwards, I will call an exemplar in the individual sense a **physical extension** of a concept and in the subset sense a **conceptual extension.** Clearly, this dichotomy of conceptual and physical extensions applies only to concrete concepts

If the extension is an abstract exemplar, that is a subset of the immediately preceding concept in a hierarchy, we can speak of extensions also as mathematical subsets, grouped by taxonomy of the internal overspecifying concepts. So we can place *garden chair*, *lawn chair* and *deck chair* into the same subset; ejector seat, car seat and pillion into a different subset.

In mathematical terms, a type of chair is a subset of chairs, possibly a wider subset than an extension, in terms of physical members. Conceptually speaking, however, in terms of possible worlds semantics, a type is not a subset of a concept per se. Possible worlds semantics is a subfield of propositional logic which relates the conceptual content of a proposition to the context in which it can or may be used[126]. We can adopt the same methodology here with the only difference remaining that we are studying the cognitive content of individual lexical items. I will use the idea of possible worlds semantics in two senses.

The first sense is a modal one and it is the one used in our present logical analysis. It refers to the possibility for a concept to restrict all the extensions of another concept. An overstuffed chair can be the set of all chairs. The overspecifying qualitative concept *overstuffed* can modify all chair subsets. This possibility can also be represented mathematically: a type is potentially a power set, that is, the set of all subsets of a concept:

> Overstuffed chair = {{ejector seat, car seat, pillion}, {garden chair, lawn chair, deck chair}, {.....}}.

All the subsets included between nested brackets are actually chairs and can potentially be conceptually restricted by the concept *overstuffed* and in this sense they belong to the power set *overstuffed chair*. This is because the overspecifying feature in a type can logically overspecify all the extensions and other types of the concept.

A type, then, can be explained in a modal sense, that is, in terms of being logically possible. So, it is logically possible for all chairs to be bell-shaped, overstuffed, comfortable[5] etc.

The second sense in which the term *possible worlds semantics* will be employed is a reifying one and it postulates the existence of an inner world in which abstract concepts have abstract extensions in much the same way that concrete concepts have physical extensions in the outside world. This is discussed in detail in section 3 of this chapter.

3:1:2:1:2:1 Conceptual definitions vs. logical definition

It is clear that the above chair definition does not apply to all chair items at a time. We have three definitional modes of concepts each corresponding to one of three conceptual paradigms: the generic definition, the extension definition and the type definition. Each of these conceptual defining modes separately does not amount to a comprehensive classical view definition of the generic concept *chair*. Furthermore, neither the central identification criterion in itself nor the peripheral identification criterion can be defining features for their respective paradigms since they are used only for identification rather than definition. A CIC is used for semantic identification of the extension as an item related to the concept intrinsically by an

---

[5] This again asserts the nominalist nature of a conceptual definition versus a logical definition of a concept.

internal process of deduction while a PIC is used in identifying the type as extrinsically related to the concept by an external process of induction. For example, the defining feature common to all chair items, extensions and types, is that of *a single person* since it is a singly sufficient and necessary feature which keeps it distinct from sofas (a seat is a piece of furniture used for seating one person). Such a defining feature exists independently of the identification criteria. This being the case, what then is the use of the CIC-PIC opposition and its consequent extension-type opposition as far as the logical definition is concerned?

The CIC is one of the intensional properties of the concept which could be defining or non-defining. Its basic function is to identify items as analytic combinations rather than synthetic ones. An example of a defining CIC is the *body parts* in the definition of medicine where a *scientific study of diseases* is not a sufficient definition since it allows for plant diseases while body parts restricts the concept to pure medicine. An example of a non-defining CIC is that of given place in the definition of chair where the defining intensional property is one person. A PIC, on the other hand is not one of the intensional properties of the concept, nor is it a defining feature. It is a peripheral feature used to identify the item as a synthetic combination

A CIC helps us form a conceptual definition of a concept by specifying the intrinsic element, which though not necessarily defining, keeps the extensions distinct from types. If we combine a conceptual definition with the intensional properties of a concept we can arrive at tight classical view definition which we can call an intensio-extensional definition. In traditional extenstional logic, the problem with extensional definitions is that they are impossible to be formed since an extensional definition necessitates the listing of all members to which the concept applies. This list is mostly impossible to find since it can be infinite as in the case of the extension of *integer*. In our present paradigm this problem is solved since the extensions of a concept are not instances but sets which are statistically finite in the lexicon of the language, like the 68 chair items (considering types as extensions in the traditional sense). Thus if we combine traditional extensional logic with the hybridized exemplar-classical views model suggested here we can argue that the extension of any concept can be finitely generated from the lexicon and will comprise both extensions and types.

Thus an intensio-extensional definition combines all the intensional properties of the thing defined besides the extensions and types of the concept generated by statistical-semantic analysis and verified by pure semantic analysis. An intensio-extensional definition of chair is, therefore, a piece of furniture used for seating one person in a given place and/or provided with a given external element.

If we fail to find an intensional defining feature, we can be sure, thanks to this intensio-extensional model, to have an extensional definition which lists the finite list of lexical items representing the concept. In such a case, i.e. in the absence of a defining feature, the ICs will insure us of a robust and concise metadefinitional language. We will not have to list all the items but rather we mention the ICs in the form of a given variable to be replaced by criterial values from the lexicon of the concept. In the above chair example, given place and given external element are replaced by values represented by the 7 identification criteria. This means that the logical definition in this new model applies to the extensions and types as conceptual entities rather than as physical instances. Thus in a worst-case scenario, dictated by the absence of a defining feature, we can have an extensional definition of each concept with a finite set provided by the lexicon thanks to the abstractive notion of exemplars furnished by the exemplar view.

3:1:2:1:3 Semantic analysis

There are three types of semantic analysis of the summary representation of concepts. These are: conceptual-semantic analysis, statistical semantic analysis and lexical-semantic analysis. Each of these types fits into a theoretical or methodological paradigm. Conceptual-semantic analysis is the type of analysis which should be conducted in the pre-processing stage, i.e. before any psychological tests can be performed. Statistical-semantic analysis is a technique which is designed to insure the accuracy of conceptual-semantic analysis. Lexical-semantic analysis is a type of production analysis, that is, an analysis of the final lexical realizations of concept in order to assess the extent to which the conceptual content is mirrored in the lexical items.

3:1:2:1:3:1 Conceptual-semantic analysis

The internal overspecifying element introduced analytically by the conceptual extension is conjunctively functional and perceptual. The place in which a chair is to be used, for example, determines its suitability for being used in that place and, therefore, its functionality. It is to be noticed that for each of the six categories of man-made objects examined, the identification criterion represents something for which the object was made. The external overspecifying element introduced by a type could be functional or nonfunctional. An example of a functional element is frying as in frying pan and an example of a nonfunctional element is easy as in easy chair. A functional element overspecifies the functional core. So, frying is but an overspecification of the abstract core of the concept pan, that is cooking, since a pan is used for cooking and frying is in semantic terms a troponym of it. When it is non-functional, it restricts the concept as a whole.

This takes us to the issue of combinations between types and extensions

3:1:2:1:3:1:1 Combinations between types and extensions

To empirically verify the assumption of holistic restriction of the concept versus partial restriction of the functional core, we can mentally restrict all the extensions of a concept by partial-functional restrictors and holistic restrictors of different types of the same concept to see whether each restriction is semantically valid. We find that holistic (non-functional) restrictors in a concept's type can, in principle at least restrict all the extensions of the concept. We can talk of *a bell car seat*, *a swivel garden chair* and *a ladder-back ejector seat*, to give but few examples. On the contrary, functional restrictors cannot possibly modify all extensions. *A feeding car seat* is a remote possibility, a *reclining saddle* is inconceivable and a *frying omellette pan* is illegally tautological. This is because functional restrictors of a type will usually clash with the functional determinant provided by the identification criterion of the extension. We cannot possibly talk of a feeding pillion, borrowing *feeding* from a feeding chair because both *pillion* and *feeding chair* are completely divergent functionally. Only when the two conceptual varieties are functionally convergent can a combination between the overspecifying functional feature of a concept's type and an extension of this concept be semantically plausible. A *reclining deck chair* is an example of this functional convergence. However, when the identification value of an extension and the functional restrictor of a type are convergent yet belong strictly to the same domain of discourse, we cannot steer safe of illegal tautology, as we have seen in the case of frying omelette pan, since frying and omelette share the same semantic field, i.e. that of cooking fried food. (I will define illegal tautology later)

3:1:2:1:3:1:2 combinations between extensions

While functional disjunctiveness prevents conceptual intersection between functional types of an object concept and its extensions, due to a functionally discordant value in the range R of the identification criterion, this functional disjunctiveness is more worthy of extensions enough to prevent any conceptual intersection between them. The overspecifying concept of an extension cannot, even in principle, restrict its sister extensions since their functional identification values are supposed to be mutually exclusive. This is simply because they refer to disjunctive objects in the real world. We cannot talk of *a garden ejector seat*, an *omelette patty pan* or a *passenger freight car*. Garden and car in the case of ejector *seat* are mutually exclusive places in the real world. And so are *passenger* and *freight* mutually exclusive loads; omelette and patty mutually exclusive foods and so on. We will see later that this rule does not apply strictly to abstract concepts as it does to concrete concepts. Figure (3) represents a simplified semantic network of the concept CHAIR:

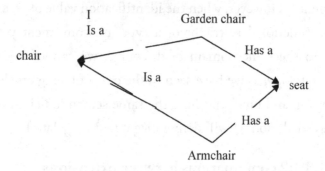

Fig 3: semantic network of the concept *chair*

It is clear that semantic networks do not show the difference between types and extensions. They represent a concept and its pertinent items wholesale. In our subsequent study of abstract concepts we use an alternative configuration, that is, conceptual networks, which highlight the distinction between extensions and types (see chapter 4)

3:1:2:1:3:2 Statistical-semantic analysis

How can we detect the identification criterion? How can we insure that the overspecifying concept is analytical rather than synthetical or the other way round without being already biased to a synthetic or analytic view? A partial answer has been given above, that is, by resorting to the criterion of holistic versus partial overspecification. If the overspecifying feature of a given subordinate concept cannot overspecify all its sister items, then this subordinate is an extension of its immediate superordinate[6] and that feature is an identification criterion serving only as an analytic partial restrictor to this extension alone. If it can, then the overspecifying feature is an external synthetic

---

[6]   By immediate superordinate I mean the generic-level category

element which has the potential for restricting each item as a whole and the concept at hand is, therefore, a type.

But this answer still presupposes that we already know what an extension is. To avoid circularity it is better to resort first to statistical semantic analysis. Our method is a simple one. First let's assume that in any conceptual combination the overspecifying concept represents an overspecification criterion. This overspecification criterion in the case of, say, *bell seat* is shape and in the case of *garden chair*, place. If just one overspecification criterion is found to be more recurrent in certain items of the concept than any of the other criteria, then it has a greater weight than all others and qualifies to be the central identification criterion. The items in which this identification criterion recurs the most number of times are assumed to be extensions while the remaining ones are assumingly types. The fact that it recurs with more items than any other single criterion does is evidence that it is constant element closely related to both the conceptual core and the identification procedures and is thus an internal overspecifier which statistical semantic analysis has brought to the surface.

For example, in the 68 chair items, the seven overspecification dimensions are those of place, shape, function, quality, added-part, movement, space. These are distributed statistically according to their occurrence as shown in table (3)

Table 3: statistical analysis of the overspecification criteria of *chair*

place	shape	movement	space	Added part	function	quality
31	7	5	4	7	4	2

We can predict from the statistics in table (3) above that none of the six overspecification criteria other than place represents a common factor between most chair items, while *place* does.

By now we can establish an important differentiation crucial to both our theoretical framework and methodology: it is that between semantic identification and perceptual identification. Our so-called identification criterion is used only in semantic identification. We intend it specifically as a means of segregating types from extensions and concept names. Perceptual identification is a process in which the identification procedure is used for category membership decisions. Semantic identification is a step which must precede empirical tests involving perceptual identification tasks by subjects.

Statistical semantic analysis helps us identify extensions and types. We identify extensions by means of weight elimination, that is, eliminating the low-weighted overspecification criteria to obatain the central identification criterion. We mean by *weight* here nothing other than the frequency of each criterion. The eliminated criteria will be those of types and we can thus identify types as the items generated from those statistically eliminated overspecification criteria. We can then check the statistical-semantic criteria by applying our "pure" semantic ones of holistic and partial restriction. If the overspecifying concept of each statistically-assumed extension cannot, even in principle, overspecify its sister extensions, then its extensionality is proven. If the overspecifying element in each statistically-assumed type can, even in principle, overspecify the extensions of the tested concept, its typicality is established. In all the six generic categories tested above, no inconsistency could be reported between the statistical-semantic and the purely semantic approaches.

3:1:2:1:3:3 Lexical-semantic analysis

We can argue, in the light of the foregoing discussions, that generic concepts are just names, abstractions that do not exist in the real world. In reality we do not have a *chair*, something which has all the identification values of chair items and the overspecifying concepts of types. In actual practice we give the extensions and types the concept names either because we don't know their names or the generic concept name is more accessible.

The identification criterion could be either lexically explicit or semantically implicit in an extension. It is explicit in a *car seat* and *garden chair*, but only implicit in *ejector seat*, for instance. A seat is provided with an ejector only to be used in a car. So the place element is assigned a greater weight here than the added-part element.

A lexically explicit identification criterion may prove to be a false one when it fails to relate the perceptual element to the functional core. For example, the content-values of *sand* and *ice* in *sandbag* and *icebag* are not related to the identification criterion of content since a sandbag and an icebag are not manufactured to perform the function of carrying sand or ice but to perform other completely different functions, i.e. those of measuring and healing, respectively.

Any given extension or type can be lexically realized either as a single word or a compound word. In the former case, the overspecifying feature is lexically embedded and can be made explicit only through a paraphrase. For example, when *a pillion* is paraphrased as *motorbike seat*, it is easy to recognize the delexicalized overspecifying feature which is but an item in the value-range of the identification criterion of place. *A roaster* is paraphrased as a roasting pan, which reveals that it is a functional type of pan since the overspecifying feature *roasting* is an external element and does not belong to the range *f* for *pan*. Componential analysis of a specific lexical item shows whether it represents a type or an extension of a given concept.

The previous arguments are aimed to give evidence for a classical view definition of concepts at the generic level together with their extensions and types. Our aim is not to provide a revised classical view model for all three levels but just to show that it is possible to give a classical view account for concepts at any of these levels. This being the target, I will not abandon the traditional, rather general terminology of" items" of a concept in the rest of this section to avoid confusion We have used the differentiating terminology of extensions and types in our present discussion for two purposes. First, for their usefulness in proving our classical view model. Second, to anticipate their subsequent usage in our major topic of abstract concepts.

3:1:3 The third critical argument

We eventually come to the third argument against the classical view. As we have seen, this argument comprises three counter arguments: the prototypicality-counter argument, transitivity counter-argument and the border-line counterargument. We discuss each one in turn.

3:1:3:1 Prototypicality counterargument

There is no guarantee that the hypothetical F0 constant suggested by Smith&Medin (1981), represents a real defining feature always listed by subjects. There is another type of real classical-view features which not only leave typicality based on non-defining features unaffected but also serve as a reasonable basis for this typicality.

These are abstract features. Like perceptual features, abstract features can be jointly necessary and sufficient and can be inherited at the subsequent levels.

3:1:3:1:1 The hierarchical basis of typicality

If similarity is the basis of typicality, a question presents itself: at which level is typicality to be sought or to be considered as relevant at all, based on this similarity? To start with, we can talk about two kinds of similarity: We will call one horizontal similarity and the other vertical similarity. What concerns us now is the former. Horizontal similarity holds between items belonging to a given category or between categories at the same level. We can call the former inside-category similarity and the latter between-category similarity. Inside-category similarity holds between exemplars, while between-category similarity holds between subsets.

This distinction is important because the first pole of it, i.e. inside-category similarity keeps the hierarchy at three levels only. For example, suppose we were talking about between-category similarity at the level *furniture*, this means that we have the superordinate *artifact* in mind and we will have to compare furniture to other subcategories of *artifact* such as clothes; weapons . . . etc. This obviously makes the hierarchy four-level. If we just restrict ourselves to inside-category similarity we will not need to go beyond a three-level hierarchy since we will just concern ourselves with the internal items of the category, not the 'external' sister-categories at the same level, which is a subordinate of an uppermost, fourth level. In other words, we will not need to talk about the typical artifact. However, There is still another reason why we will not talk about the typical artifact. Items belonging under a category at a fourth level will be so distinctive that it would be difficult to find a basis of similarity between them. Having now slimmed the hierarchy to three levels, the question: at which of these three levels is the basis of typicality to be sought? remains still a valid question.

3:1:3:1:1:1 The Superordinate level

We cannot talk about typicality at the superordinate level since items within a category at this level are still so distinctive that it is hard to find a sound common basis of similarity. Lack of a common basis of similarity could be due to the absence of an abstract functional core whereby concrete features or dimensions are constrained. For example, there are no regular features common between all furniture items which are related to a common functional core. There could be accidental features these items have in common which they also share with other non-furniture items, such as having *legs*. Suppose we wrongly included *chair* among *home appliances*, subjects may include in their feature list *having legs* as a feature common to chairs and some home appliances, but we know that this similarity is hardly relevant to category membership. In order for a point of similarity to be related to category membership—and in turn—to typicality, it must be constrained by a common abstract, imperceptible feature.

In our paradigm case of *chair*, the functional feature of seating makes the feature *have legs* relevant in the categorization of an item as a chair and then in deciding that an item is a typical chair on account of similarity with other chairs in this feature. Simply chairs must have legs in order to be used for seating and in order to be rightly defined as chairs. In the absence of an abstract feature as a basis of similarity, what has been said about the irrelevance of concrete features can also apply to dimensions. In our present furniture example, the dimension of size in and of itself cannot be considered as a common basis of similarity since furniture items are so diversified in size. Even if a chair is similar to many furniture items in terms of size, this similarity has to do with an ontological similarity it shares with many non-furniture items rather than to its exclusive membership in the furniture category.

At a superordinate level, even abstract functional features may fail to constrain the items to a set of similar objects. Let us pick an example. It is the concept *weapon*. Though the abstract functional feature common to all weapons is that of "being used to inflict physical harm", it hardly constrains them to a set of regularly similar objects. Embedded in this feature is the dimension *degree of harm*. Even in a graded dimensional scale ranging from light to moderate up to severe harm, weapons are still widely disparate in size, shape within the same range of inflictable harm. In a moderate harm range, we can find a set of items that cannot be visually reduced to a set of regular perceptual features. We will find at this range, for example, a shotgun, a penknife and a catapult, which are widely dissimilar in terms of their perceptual features. Tanks and bombs, though they can inflict a symmetrical degree of harm, are hardly similar in their featural or dimensional properties. Thus degree of harm alone, though abstract and functional, is not constraining. Suppose, then, that subjects listed for say, gun, features that were later found to be present in many other weapons. For example, it has a blade like a knife, a butt like a pistol and a barrel like an artillery. Can we say, then, on the basis of these shared topographical features that gun is the typical weapon? Indeed, in the absence of an abstract feature which constrains the concrete features, such kind of similarity can hardly be a basis for typicality. In other words, accidental similarity between items 'inside' a category at a given level which also holds between these items and other inherently dissimilar ones should not count towards typicality ratings unless it is regularized by an abstract constraining feature. This feature is not likely to be found at the superordinate level.

3:1:3:1:1:2 The Lower Level

Category items at a lower level are so non-distinctive that they hardly need an abstract feature to harmonize them. They already form a symmetrical set. This holds true of categories of both natural and man-made objects alike. Trouts, to a nonexpert eye, are so indistinguishable from one another that it would be ridiculous to ask people to single out the typical trout. Similarly for man-made objects, it would be unreasonable to give subjects who are not furniture experts pictures of armchair designs and ask them to tell which design represents the typical armchair. Perhaps, no one of them may have seen more than a single armchair in his entire life. More unreasonable still would be a calculation of the typical armchair based on similarity of armchair features listed by these subjects. Unlike the superordinate level, it is symmetricality rather than dissimilarity or accidental similarity which is responsible for the irrelevance of typicality at the lower level of categorization.

It becomes obvious, then, that the middle level of categorization is the level at which typicality has any significance at all.

3:1:3:1:1:1:3 The Middle Level

Returning to our chair example, we can see now how the abstract *seating* feature exemplifies the fact that such a feature is not found at the superordinate level of furniture and that it has no significance for typicality at the lower level. Only at the middle-chair level can it be recognized and found to be important for producing sound typicality effects. As for the *weapon* example, in which the abstract dimension of causing harm failed as a constraining feature at the superordinate level-and also at other subsequent levels, a constraining abstract feature can be found only at the middle level. This feature can be called *the method of inflicting harm*. It redistributes the widely asymmetrical set of weapons at the superordinate level to more symmetrical taxonomical sets at the middle level so that we have a gun set, a tank set, a missile set, a sharp tool set . . . etc according to the method of inflicting harm. For example, guns kill by shooting, artillery by shelling, bombs by direct explosion, sharp tools by stabbing and so on. Inside each set we will find that, thanks to the abstract *method* constraint, items assume closer dimensional proportions in terms of size, the degree of harm and also closer featural properties related to shape, material . . . etc.

Thus the abstract *method* feature assigned to each set is related to the concrete features and dimensions of items in the set to the extent that each feature is befitted to a certain method of inflicting harm. Knives are sharp so as to be effective wounding devices. Pistols and rifles are metallic so that they can stand the heat of the exploding bullets and can thus be effective in firing them quickly and effectively at the target when the weapon is triggered by its holder, and so on.

Now if we set about the task of selecting the typical and atypical items for each middle-level set based on their degree of similarity to other items in the same set, we can be sure that the typicality effects we obtain are actually related to category-specific similarity and not to general ontological similarity. The typical item in such a case will be representative of the interplay between the abstract feature and the concrete features-in other words, it will be truly representative of the category.

It is our contention that property inheritance is behind the stabilizing inside-category similarity at the middle level which serves as the logical basis of typicality. The general feature *used for supporting*, though hardly constraining or regularizing at the superordinate level, is inherited from furniture by the middle-level concept *chair* only to be constrained by the seating feature which regularizes chair items into a harmonious set at the middle level. Subcategories of weapons inherit the abstract feature *inflicting harm* from weapons and constrain it by the method-specific feature suitable for each subcategory. Thus each method-specific feature constrains the features and dimensions to a single middle-level subset. Of course all the items in the subset inherit this feature and may constrain it by another abstract feature and so on. Now if subjects in a typicality test selected *rifle* as the typical gun due to its featural similarity with other guns, this will be a meaningful selection to us because it is methodically and functionally similar to other guns.

In short, family resemblance is the true basis of typicality. But without an abstract, constraining feature; this family resemblance turns into ontological resemblance, that is accidental resemblance shared between family members which is also shared between members of other families without a common ground for this sharedness. To be more accurate, we cannot obtain refined taxonomical families without finding a truly harmonizing abstract feature. This abstract feature plays its constraining role best at the middle level but is inherited from a superordinate level at which it does not appear due to unconstrained similarity between the taxonomically similar items and ontological similarity between taxonomically dissimilar items at this level.

For concepts of natural objects, there is no need to search for an abstract feature. Accidental resemblance between natural categories is far less than that holding between categories of man-made objects. Birds share far less features with mammals than chairs do with tables, for example[7]. Ontological features are constrained by category-specific features rather than by any external abstract ones. A bird's having two legs, a feature it may share with a squirrel, is constrained by the dimension of size since the only two-legged creature with bird size will be just a bird. A robin may be of the same size as a cat, but other distinctive features are sufficient to make the robin set an ontologically differentiated one without any need for an abstract constraint. On the contrary, a chair does not possess such redeeming attributes, whether features or dimensions, as can be sufficient to prevent ontological resemblance with tables or cupboards. In the presence of an abstract seating feature, the dimensional feature *size 3*, for example, on a scaled size dimension assigned to *artifacts*, will bring into the mind only chairs, but without this abstract feature it may bring into the mind an undifferentiated jumble of artifacts with this size.

3:1:3:2 Transitivity counterargument

---

[7]   I mean by features in this context species-specific features rather than general biological features shared by all living organisms such as Breathe+ or Multiply+.

Now it is time to discuss the notion of vertical similarity since it has a lot to bear on the account we provide of cases of intransitivity within the framework of the classical view. By vertical similarity is meant similarity holding between items at a given level and those at higher levels. This similarity decreases as we go down a hierarchy in a binary fashion so that a lower-level category is more similar to a middle-level category than this middle level category is to a superordinate level. Armchairs and car seats are more similar to chairs than they are to furniture and than chairs are to furniture. This is because the abstract functional bond which relates armchairs and car seats to chairs is far stronger than the one that relates them to furniture.

The example of intransitivity provided by Hampton (1982) fails to differentiate between the conceptual extension and the physical extension. Subjects did not judge Big Bin to be furniture though they judged it to be *clock* and *clock* to be furniture because for *clock* Big Bin is a unique physical instance, that is, a physical extension. Yet for furniture Big Bin is not a physical extension and clearly it is not a subset either. Only *clock* represents an abstract subset, and is therefore a conceptual extension of furniture. Besides, Big Bin is on a borderline between *clock and structure*.

Borderline counterargument

The question which poses itself is: if the concepts are incomplete, is it because they are inherently so or because our knowledge of them is incomplete; in other words, is our cognition or our metacognition to blame for the fuzziness of concepts? In my opinion, the latter is to blame. In order to make sure that our cognitive definition of a concept is complete, we should first construct a metacognitive definition of this concept through a full-fledged semantic analysis. Then we can proceed to verify our intuitions by resorting to semantic tasks involving different subjects to see to what extent our metacognitive, consciously constructed concepts correspond to our psychologically constructed ones.

In our present case of borderline concepts, conceptual incompleteness can be overhauled linguistically by taking recourse to what we can call *syntagmatic similarity between lexical items*. Some lexical items possess a considerable degree of similarity in their lexical environment though they are paradigmatically wide apart, i.e. they belong to different natural taxonomies. For example, birds, flies and airplanes share a lot of contextual delimiters. A bird can "fly", "hover" and "land" on the ground and so can a fly and an airplane. At the same time, this syntagmatic similarity is a result of paradigmatic featural similarity between birds, flies, and airplanes. The three categories can be assigned the features FLY+ and Winged+.

But birds, flies and planes represent an extreme case. They do not represent borderline cases, yet they serve to illustrate what we mean by syntagmatic similarity. The example of a *sink* provided earlier by Hampton (1979) can serve as a moderate case of syntagmatic similarity. A sink behaves lexically like a container, though conceptually it is not a container per se. You can "fill" it, "empty" it and "drain" it. It can also be "full to the brim". It still retains some container features such as hollowness and holdability. So we can assign sinks the feature container+. This feature, combined with the functional feature "used for washing" can form a classical view definition of a sink as "a container with a tap and a drain used for washing things in a kitchen or bathroom". It is not difficult to discover that the feature container+ is common to many other sanitary containers such as a wash basin and a bath. This feature, then, can be transformed into an exclusive conceptual category called sanitary *containers*. This category can be considered semantically as a subordinate of the general container taxonomy. It will be the task of the empirical psychologist to verify the psychological validity of this semantic taxonomy by asking his subjects to rate different sink items as containers or noncontainers.

The problem with Hampton's task is that he chose the wrong semantic taxonomy i.e. that of kitchen utensils as a criterion against which to ask his subjects to categorize a kitchen sink. Such a choice must be preceded by close semantic analysis of the target and the probes. It is my assumption that any ontologically symmetrical set of items will be also semantically symmetrical. Utensils do not represent an ontologically symmetrical set: they can come about as sharp tools like knives and forks or they can be containers like pans and dishes, and besides, they are also functionally asymmetrical. The reverse of this assumption holds true: any semantically symmetrical set is also ontologically symmetrical. But we should be alert to what type of semantic similarity we are building our choice upon, i.e. whether it is paradigmatic, natural similarity or syntagmatic, lexically-based similarity. Even the latter, as we have noted, must be based on some common paradigmatic features between naturally divergent categories. Syntagmatically similar items then can be said to form lexical paradigms to which we can safely fit our assumingly border-line concepts when the natural paradigms fail us.

A final note of caution should be highlighted. We must be aware of the difference between syntagmatic similarity between paradigmatically different items and general ontological similarity related to all-taxonomy ontology. For example, the fact that pets can be "kept" at home and so can machines is not sufficient evidence that both pets and machines form lexical paradigms in the sense meant here in our conceptual jargon. They form lexical-semantic paradigms in the sense that they can pick up some shared selectional restrictions. Conceptually, however, they have nothing to do with each other. This means that the criterion of lexical paradigms is not an absolute one. If syntagmatic similarity is not constrained by a certain threshold of paradigmatic similarity, such as that holding between bird and plane, then our so-called lexical paradigms cannot be used as a last resort for category membership[8]. They will be in this case "linguistic paradigms" only, not conceptual ones. In other words, we should be able to judge whether lexical paradigms are lexical-semantic or lexical-conceptual. To conclude, if the interdependent relationship between language and concepts is not given due attention by psychologists, we will be confronted by all kinds of border-line cases in real-world concepts. This deals an unjustified blow to the classical view.

---

[8] We can also argue that functional features can be a basis for forming natural lexical paradigms based on syntagmatic similarity. For example, both camels and cars can be driven, and can be items in a taxonomy for means of transportation.

Chapter 4

Abstract Concepts

4:1 Overview

The three modes of concepts discussed so far are synthetic conceptual combinations (types), abstract exemplars (extensions), and concept names. They have been discussed in so far as they are related to concrete concepts. This discussion serves two purposes for our present research. The first purpose is that of using them analogically to analyse abstract concepts. It is a major assumption here that the link between the concrete world and the inner world can be established by using the same paradigm in dissecting the content of both the abstract concepts and the concrete ones. We will see in this chapter that even perceptual features can be found in some non-concrete concepts such as action concepts: some actions refer to material events which can be identified perceptually and analysed semantically in concrete, reifying terms.

The second purpose is related to conceptual transfer of abstract nouns in English-Arabic translation. It is assumed that synthetic combinations require more processing by the mind of the translator while analytic combinations require less time to translate since they are already inside the cognitive content of the concept. This assumption will be tested empirically in chapter 5.

In the discussion of concrete concepts, the term "abstract" was used in one sense, that is *general* or related to an abstraction; we used it mainly to refer to abstract exemplars introduced by the exemplar theory and we changed the term *abstract exemplar* to conceptual extension to suit our methodological purposes. Now in our discussion of abstract concepts, we draw again on the concept of abstract exemplar yet in a different sense. Here *abstract* means two things: 1) general 2) non-concrete. So an extension of an abstract concept is *general* in the sense that it is a category of mental objects and in this respect it is similar to a concrete concept. For example, mathematics is an extension of science and is at the same time an 'abstract' set of other minor disciplines such as algebra, geometry, etc. The extension of an abstract concept is nonconcrete because it has no signification in the real world. An abstract concept has no physical extensions the way concrete concepts have. And it is mainly in this respect that it is different from a concrete concept. So the term conceptual extension is no longer applicable here since it was used to differentiate between exemplars as abstract sets in the mind and as physical extensions in the world. Thus the term *extension* alone will be used in the case of abstract concepts since they have no physical counterparts.

Extensions of abstract concepts exist in the inner world of cognition. In this inner world the counterparts of conceptual extensions are mental subcategories including abstract objects. For example, mathematics, an extension of science, is a subset subsuming other sciences such as algebra, geometry, calculus . . . etc. The counterparts of physical extensions in the inner world are what we can call *cognitive instances*. A Cognitive instance, by analogy to a unique physical extension of a concrete concept, is an extension of an abstract concept which does not have the dual nature of being an abstract set and a unique instance at the same time[9]. Examples of cognitive instances are English, French, Persian as instances of the concept LANGUAGE. Similarly, Islam and Christianity are cognitive instances of RELIGION. Such concepts as religion and language have no subset extensions in the inner world. Natural language, artificial language, divine religion and natural religion, as it transpires in the next chapter, are just *types* of *language* and *religion*.

4:1:1 Abstract concepts as abstract entities

The term abstract entity is used in philosophy to refer to concepts in contradistinction to the terms *ideas* and *universals*. In this sense, an abstract entity is a general term for any indirectly observable entities such as classes, functions, numbers and relations[127] The philosopher Katz defends the existence of abstract entities against charges of nominalists who denied the existence of any such entities by analogical reference to physical science. According to Katz (1966), physical scientists say that certain microentities are unobservable, but what gives their claims about such entities empirical content is that they connect the postulated existence of such things with certain observable phenomena through a complex chain of deductive relations. Hence, "scientific method offers us a straightforward way of establishing the existence of unobservable entities and processes, one which there is no legitimate reason to

---

[9] Big Bin serves, as an extension of clock, serves as an example of a unique physical extension (instance) of a concrete concept.

preclude from linguistics"[128]. We will take up Katz's views a step further to lay our hands on what observable phenomena in language underlie abstract entities.

4:1:2 Abstract concepts versus abstract entities: a paradigm shift

Our first aim in the current endeavour is to establish a linguistic perspective of abstract entities which keeps them distinct from abstract concepts. An abstract concept is a concept of a non-concrete object which has an intension in the mind and extensions in the inner world of cognition. So, extensions of the concept SCIENCE are physics, mathematics, chemistry, those of mathematics are algebra, arithmetic, geometry and so on. Abstract concepts themselves do not differ in their degree of abstractness (in the sense of non-concreteness) though they do differ in the degree of generality, so that ideology is more generic than socialism, socialism more generic than communism and so on, as we noted earlier.

Extensions of the concept JOB in the inner world are not John's job, a good job, or Mark's profession; they are engineering, carpentry, programming etc. (A) Job is an individuated realization of the concept on the same generic level. From now on I will call such individuated realization of a concept at the same level an *abstract entity*. No explicit reference is made to abstract entities as such in the literature. However, an implicit reference can be found in Haliday's enlightening discussion on the difference between text and a text. While text (without article) is seen as a process, a text is regarded as a product or an entity. This maps well, as will become more obvious, to the differentiation presented here between abstract concepts and abstract entities.

4:1:2:1 Abstract entities versus concrete entities

An abstract entity such as [a] science is an individuated mental realization of the abstract concept SCIENCE. Abstract entities are extensionally opaque in such a way as concrete entities are. Concrete entities are just another name for the physical extensions of concrete concepts. Thus in so much that a physical cat is an extension of the concept *cat* in the real world and so represents a terminal node in a representational line linking the concept *cat* to the physical extension *cat*, the abstract entity *a science* is a terminal node in a branch of a hierarchy tree which links the concept *science* to the abstract entity *a science*, bearing in mind that the abstract entity is at the same level of the concept while the physical extension is at a lower level. Thus the only point of convergence between the physical extension and the abstract entity is that both are extensionally opaque. Conceptually, we cannot generate any further extensions from the physical extension. Similarly, we cannot generate from the abstract entity any abstract extensions. So a *physics* is not an extension of *a science* but a particularized version of *physics*. *A chemistry* does not subsume one or the other of the two extensions of chemistry, i.e. organic chemistry and inorganic chemistry, but is rather a particularized version of chemistry in a general sense.

The difference between an extension of an abstract concept and an abstract realization of that concept (i.e. an abstract entity) is that while the former has a "unique existence" in the inner world of cognition, the latter is an individuated mental replica of the concept which is realizable in the individuated language form we term *entitive noun*. Before we pursue this point, it would be useful to examine the nature of lexical items on the scale of abstractness and concreteness.

4:1:3 Abstract versus concrete speech elements

According to the theory of extensionalism, concrete lexical items are those lexical items that have as their referents concrete objects[129]. They can be nouns, adjectives or verbs. Nouns such as *dog, man, table, sugar* have direct referents. An Abstract lexical item such as *imagination* has as its direct referents some class of abstract objects which constitute acts of imagination[130].

What, then, about such words as *happy, great, large, extensive* . . . etc? These words cannot be said to have direct referents in their own; they refer to things only when they describe them, so in the phrase *a happy man*, *happy* refers to man imparting to him the state of being *happy*; as *tall* in *a tall tree* refers to *tree* by imparting to it the attribute of being tall and so on. Thus the indirect referent of the adjective is the direct referent of the noun this adjective qualifies. Likewise, words like *believe, eat, hit*, do not have direct referents, i.e. objects, abstract, or concrete, to which they refer in a one-to-one relationship of reference; what they refer to is indirectly determined by the actions or events they describe. Their abstractness or concreteness is determined by these actions or events, according as they imply physical actions such as *kill, eat, kiss*; mental acts such as *think, contemplate* or emotional states such as *love, hate*. Thus, nouns are the most straightforward speech elements as far as their referential scope is concerned. Perhaps this is the reason why standard grammar textbooks normally talk of abstract nouns and concrete nouns, but not of abstract adjectives or concrete adjectives, nor concrete verbs and abstract verbs.

4:1:3:1 Conceptual nouns and entitive nouns

An important assumption is that noun countability is not just an arbitrary grammatical feature of lexical items, but is a very real representation of conceptual content[131]. In this light, abstract nouns can be divided into two broad categories: conceptual nouns and entitive nouns. A conceptual noun is an abstract uncountable noun that represents the physical realization in word-form of an abstract concept. It may denote a state, attribute, event, ideology or creative domain:

> State: happiness, anger
> Attribute: intelligence, stupidity
> Event: death /marriage
> Ideology: Religion > Christianity > Protestantism,
>   communism
> Creative domain: Science > mathematics > algebra

The arrows show the hierarchical IS-A links between abstract nouns and, correspondingly, between abstract concepts.

In order for a noun to represent an abstract concept and be thus considered a conceptual noun, it must satisfy the following conditions:

A) It must be an abstract noun
B) It must be uncountable
C) It must be generic in scope i.e. denoting a general concept such as "freedom", "politics", "religion", Marxism (i.e. in contrast to a freedom, a religion or a marxist attitude, for instance)

C) It must be able to stand alone as subject of a predicate without any pre-modifier in a general statement as in (3) and (4).

  (3) Love is sweet

  (4) Democracy is an illusion

An entitive noun is a countable abstract noun which represents the physical realization in word-form of an abstract entity. In order for a noun to be considered an entitive noun, it must:

A) be a countable, abstract noun

B) be unable to stand alone without a premodifier; (5) and (6) are thus ungrammatical[10]

  (5) I like idea *

  (6) I have opinion*

C) be unable to stand alone (without a pre-modifier) as a subject in a general statement. Thus (7) is ungrammatical too.

  (7) Idea is the prime mover of achievement*

D) be specific in scope, that is, referring to a specific trait, event, entity . . . etc as in (8), (9) and (10)

  (8) He has an amazing ability to solve technical problems.

  (9) He has really committed a folly

  (10) That's a scientific miracle.

In (8), (9) and (10) above, *ability, folly* and *miracle* refer to a specific trait, event, respectively. Abstract entities differ from abstract concepts not in the degree of generality, but in the degree of abstractness

---

[10] Ungrammatical here does not refer to the Chomskyan notion of unacceptability but rather to grammatical incorrectness per se.

(i.e. nonconcreteness) and therefore the nouns representing them reflect this difference. Thus an abstract entitive noun reveals a lesser degree of nonconcreteness than a conceptual noun does, since the former can be used in a more "concrete" lexical environment together with "concrete" lexical items. You can "give" an idea, "write" some ideas or "exchange" ideas, but you can't read, write, give or exchange *idealism*, for example. Such is the cognitive operation known as *reification*. By the semantic effect of this operation, "the referent becomes conceptualized as an object or a mass, one that can participate in many of the same actions-such as being given or gotten-as a physical quantity"[132]

4:1:4 Extensions of abstract concepts

In our previous discussion of concrete concepts we gave a categorial exemplar the term *conceptual extension* and an individual exemplar the term *physical extension*. According to the exemplar view, *abstract exemplar* covers both terms. Now that there is no scope for physical extensions the qualifying adjective *conceptual* will be dispensed with. We can talk of an extension both as an individual exemplar of an abstract concept and a subcategory of it. Generally speaking, extension of an abstract concept can be defined as the set of conceptual entities in the inner world of cognition to which the intensional properties of that concept apply. Thus, in so much as my caboodle, John's dog and Ali's retriever are entities in the real world to which the concept "dog" is applicable, so are *physics*, *medicine*, *mathematics* individual instances of the concept "science" in the world of cognition.

4:1:4:1 Abstract concept Vs concrete concept extension

Extensions of abstract concepts and conceptual extensions of concrete concepts share two important properties, that of being an abstraction in the mind and that of being a subset. These two properties are far from being shared between extensions of abstract concepts and physical extensions of concrete concepts.

The difference between extensions of abstract concepts and physical extensions of concrete concepts remains that while the latter are entities, the former are concepts subcategorized from higher level concepts, subcategorization being the process of consecutive arriving at lower hierarchical organizational levels from which other concepts or, as it were, conceptual entities are extensionally generated.

The result is that each extensional child will share its immediate parent the latter's basic intensional properties and the same parent will in turn share the one just above it its basic intensional properties too so that the terminal concept (which can potentially ramify) will inherit all the intensional properties of the higher levels in the hierarchical order, which is in keeping with the property inheritance principle. For instance, *pediatrics* is a member of the "medicine family" which is concerned with the scientific study of child disease. So pediatrics is a science, a "medicine "and ultimately, a creative domain. Another difference between extensions of abstract concepts and physical extensions of concrete concepts is that the latter are extensionally opaque; a physical dog is a terminal node in the Dog (concept)—>dog (extension) relationship, while "medicine" is not a terminal node in the science—>medicine hierarchy.

4:1:4:2 Extensions as cognitive instances

By their very extensional nature, extensions of abstract concepts can be individual instances which, by analogy to concrete, real-world physical extensions, should not generate any further instances; yet it is their categorial nature which makes them able to ramify into other subcategories or, rather, subconcepts. There is some sort of extensions which have a unitary nature, that is, they either cannot be subdivided into other extensions or can have only vertically asymmetrical ones, that is, ones that violate the transitivity principle. They are the abstract analogues to unique physical extensions. We will call them, as we decided earlier, *cognitive* instances. Examples of cognitive instances are the extensions of the abstract concept *language*, and those of the abstract concept *religion*. Extensions of language are the set of all known languages, i.e. urdu, Arabic, English . . . etc, which do not subcategorize into further instances[11]. The extensions of religion, which are the set of all religions can have extensions of their own yet their extensions are not bound by a transitive relationship to the superordinate concept For example, we can conclude from a skimming of the classification of religions in the Encyclopedia of religion that Catholicism and Protestantism are extensions of Christianity but they are not extensions of religion. Similarly, Shiism and Sunnism are not religions in their own right, though each can be considered an extension of the concept Islam. This is why we consider them as vertically asymmetrical with the superordinate concept.

4:1:4:3 Lexical representation of extensions

Table (4) gives some examples of abstract concepts together with their extension, which represents the conceptual level, and their physical realization in conceptual nouns (CNs) or Entitive nouns (ENs).

---

[11]   Colloquial English and Standard Arabic, for instance are just types of language, not extensions of it

concept	extension	Physical realization (PR)			
science	Physics, Maths, chemistry,	CN	Equiv	EN	Equiv
		science		A science	A discipline
language	English, Arabic,	language		A language	A tongue
religion	Islam/Christianity	religion	Faith	A religion	A faith
job	Engineering, carpentry			A job	A profession
chemistry		chemistry			

Table (4): abstract concepts and their physical realizations in English.

As table (4) shows, some abstract concepts have as their extensions in the cognitive world abstract exemplars which can be both subsets and instances, according to the exemplar view. Other concepts have as their extensions in the inner world concepts which are only instances but do not form subsets in a classical view sense. Examples of these are *language* and *religion* whose extensions are the set of all named languages and religions. The third major cell to the right represents the physical realization level (PR). The five concepts provided can be lexically realized in conceptual nouns. The only exception is that of *job*, which has no CN realization. With the exception of *chemistry*, the other four concepts have EN realizations. It can also be noticed from the data in table (3) that equivalents (i.e. full synonyms) of Cns are rare while En equivalents are more frequent. Fig (4) illustrates the complex relations between the conceptual and the realizational level.

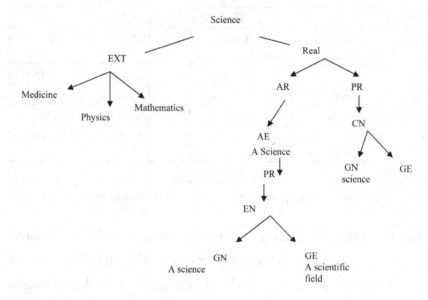

Fig (4): A conceptual and lexical configuration of the concept *science*.

Figure (4) represents a sample configuration of an abstract concept, namely the concept SCIENCE. The Extension node (Ext) represents the cognitive level of mind. The realization node (Real) represents the realizational level of language. The abstract realization node (AR) represents a hypothetical cognitive level that helps to explain the existence of entitive nouns in language as lexical encapsulations of abstract entities.

The abstract entity (AE), like neutrons in physics, is a hypothetical idea which serves as a cognitive basis, as we have just indicated, for explaining the existence of entitive nouns in language as indirect physical realizations of abstract concepts as opposed to conceptual nouns which are direct physical realizations of these concepts. Thus AE is the intermediary state between the conceptual level of mind and the realizational level of language.

The relationship between the AR node and the secondary PR node in Figure (4) is, therefore, not a hierarchical relation of dominance, but one of intermediacy with the AE node acting as an intermediator. Conceptual nouns (CNs) do not need such intermediation to justify their existence since they are direct realizations of abstract concepts. Since abstract concepts stand solitary in the mind in abstraction from real-world material adjuncts, similarly conceptual nouns can stand alone in language unfettered by concrete adjuncts such as pre-modifiers or determiners and are thus considered the "lexical "counterparts of abstract concepts.

GN stands for generic name, i.e. generic name of the concept while GE stands for generic equivalent, that is, a synonym of the concept at the generic level. Since an abstract entity is a mental recursion of the concept, so an entitive noun has a generic name identical to the generic name of the conceptual noun as can be seen in the secondary physical realization tree branching from the AE node of *science* in figure (4)

4:1:5 Types of abstract concepts

Needless to say, the abstract-perceptual dichotomy is no longer relevant in the identification of extensions of abstract concepts now that all features are "abstract". The question now is: what criteria can we use to sort out extensions of abstract concepts from their types, if any? Research into abstract concepts reveals that though there are no general criteria for identifying extensions and types of abstract concepts, some of the criteria employed in identifying the extensions and types of concrete concepts can be used in identifying those of abstract concepts alongside other criteria specific to each taxonomy of abstract concepts. The conceptual core of each abstract concept is discovered by employing criteria related to a given taxonomy of abstract concepts to which the concept at hand belongs. In section 4-3 a detailed taxonomy of abstract concepts is provided in which each taxonym forms its extensions and types in a special way, whether independently or in relation to other taxonyms. For example, there are *system concepts* and *discipline concepts*. Each extension of a discipline concept has an investigative relation with a corresponding component of a system concept. For instance, each extension of the concept *linguistics* such as *semantics*, *syntax* and *morphology* is concerned with a component of the language system, i.e. meaning, syntx and word structure, respectively.

For the time being, we can draw a general line of demarcation between extensions and types of abstract concepts. A type of an abstract concept is an overspecification of this concept by means of another concept which restricts its intensional properties and extensional range. Thus, NATURAL LANGUAGE, for example, is an overspecified version of LANGUAGE by means of the concept of "naturalness", but not an extension of it the way French, English, Arabic, and Swahili . . . etc are. The distinction between types and extensions can be made clearer when we employ the criterion of partial versus holistic restriction which we used with concepts of man-made objects. The usually lexically explicit overspecifying concept in a given type can potentially specify all the extensions of the typified concept. Examining, for example, the concept MEDICINE, we find that *aviation medicine* is a type of medicine simply because there is no logical barrier to having, say, aviation *dermatology* or aviation *ophthalmology*. Yet an often lexically embedded overspecifying concept of an extension does not, in principle, overspecify the other extensions belonging under the same superordinate concept. We neither have nor can visualise a gynecological ophthalmology?? Or, more absurdly, hepatic gynecology. Dermatological venerology, or pediatric ophthalmology, however, are not as remote.

This is due to the fact that in the case of such medicine extensions as *ophthalmology* and *hepatology*, the embedded overspecifying concept is that of a "study of one of the parts of the body", and these parts are themselves mutually exclusive in the real world. Such mutual exclusiveness does not hold between dermatology and several other medicine extensions since the part with which it is concerned, i.e. the skin, permeates all the other outer bodily organs. This being the case, we can argue for *dermatology* as a type candidate. This situation is even clearer in the case of Pediatrics, which is indeed also more of a type of MEDICINE than an extension of it. The embedded restricting (i.e. overspecifying) concept in pediatrics (i.e. Child disease) can logically restrict (i.e. overspecify) the other extensions of medicine so that we can visualise a paediatric cardiology, pediatric hepatology. etc. Thus semantic analysis by employing the holistic versus partial restriction technique shows the analytic or synthetic nature of medicine items. This technique, as we will see later, proves successful in sifting the extensions and types of abstract concepts.

4:2 A cognitive theory of definitions

Formulating a general theory of definitions is crucial to understanding the processing of concepts in the monolingual and the bilingual mind. This is because the Central Identification Criterion (CIC) in concepts of man-made objects and abstract concepts is a basic factor in forming a tight definition of such concepts. It is at the same time the factor which determines that an item is an extension and sorts it out from types. Furthermore, definitions are an integral part of the processing hypothesis since each definition forms a metacognitive shell of the cognitive data to be processed.

A strict classical theory definition can be arrived at only through semantic analysis of the lexical items which realize the concept we want to define. Detecting a concept core, as we have seen, allows us to reach a definition which defies the counterclaims of fuzzy logic.

For natural world concepts, the concept core is one of the identification procedures, an identification procedure which functions as a defining feature of the set being defined, such as barking in dogs and meowing in cats. Thus it marks the defined set off from other sets and comprises all the members, bearing in mind that what we mean by "member" is conceptual member, rather than physical instance. The reason why the concept core in natural world concepts is one of the identification procedures rather than an abstract feature embedding an identification criterion is that natural world concepts don't have an abstract functional core which divides the items statistically into extensions and types. The extension-type dichotomy results from the presence of intrinsic elements embedded within the concept and externalized through semantic analysis, and other external elements that form compound concepts by combination with the original concept. This is not the case with natural world objects since their parts are all intrinsic by force of nature and they do not have externally added parts through artificial combination.

As for man-made objects, formulating a solid definition depends on detecting a singly necessary and sufficient defining feature. This defining feature can be an abstract functional feature expressed by a gerund or an element embedded in its propositional content. We call the gerundive functional feature in such a case the concept core.

In case the concept core fails to produce a defining feature, we resort to identification criteria that help us form an intensio-extensional definition which overhauls the lack of a defining feature by generating the finite set of conceptual extensions from the intensional properties of the concept which are constrained by these criteria.

Formulating an intensio-extensional definition in the case of an abstract concept will be much easier than in the case of a concrete concept for a variety of reasons. First, ontological similarity between items pertaining to the same category is unlikely in the case of abstract concepts. This similarity may obstruct the way to finding necessary and sufficient features due to an intersection of features across categories in the same domain. For example, sofa and chair as furniture items share a lot of features, while chemistry and medicine as items of science share very few features. Second, in many cases, items belonging to a category of abstract concepts are very limited in number and therefore can be included in a short list that represents an extensional definition of that conceptual category. The same analytic procedures used in the case of concrete concepts can be applied here in order to reach a solid definition of an abstract concept. The concept core can be arrived at through a decompositional analysis of the lexical items representing the concept in the lexicon.

4:2:1 Conceptual definition of abstract concepts

We can now differentiate between two types of definition of abstract concepts: logical and conceptual. A logical definition has to cover intensionally all the items of the concept defined by a set of necessary and sufficient features and/or extensionally by listing all the extensions of the concept, in the wider sense which includes extensions and types. For example, a logical definition of medicine allows for all medicine items, be they extensions or types. So extensions such as hepatology and cardiology and types such as prophylactic medicine and aviation medicine have to be covered by an intensio-extensional definition of Medicine.

A conceptual definition of an abstract concept covers only the conceptual extensions, i.e. those items which are analytically related to the concept through a central identification criterion. Types are excluded from this definition since they are synthetic combinations. A conceptual definition as such is tailored to abstract concepts since it helps to draw conceptual lines of demarcation between their members, without any detriment to logical definition. This is because members of abstract categories are not tangible entities in the real world which are lurking here and there waiting for a logical definition to put them in one definitional basket. Rather, they are mental constructs built up by the practical mind according to our degree of knowledge and how we perceive them analytically or synthetically. For example defining chemistry as the science which is concerned with the study of organic and inorganic matter is a self-sufficient definition of chemistry though it covers only two subdisciplines of chemistry: organic and inorganic chemistry. The other three ones, analytic chemistry, physical chemistry and bio chemistry are just types not chemistry per se;they are intersections between chemistry and other sciences. No logician in such a case has the right to tell us to think otherwise on grounds that these three types have to be included in the definition. We cannot define chemistry as a science concerned with the study of organic matter and inorganic matter and/or using the analytic methods of statistics and /or forming an interdisciplinary field with physics or biology, merely to include analytic chemistry, biological chemistry and physical chemistry. This will be a fuzzy definition since all sciences use statistical analytic methods and form interdisciplinary fields with one another. Yet any logician has every right to blame us if our definition of chair fails to encompass such types as ladder-back or the swivel chair, though it is quite clear that added part and movement are not essential to a chair definition. This is simply because a ladder-back chair, though a type, is not a mental construct but a tangible entity on the ground of the real world and excluding it will do harm to a logical definition.

4:2:2 Linguistic analysis of definitional content

In the study of concepts of man-made objects, it could be observed that the abstract functional core is lexically realized as a gerund whose tenseless vp consists of Verb+object+optional complement. The CIC and the defining feature can fill in syntactic positions in the argument structure of of the vp. For example, in the definition of chair as a piece of furniture used for seating one person in a given place, the defining feature *one person* falls in the object position while the CiC fills in the complement position as object of the preposition in the pp *in a given place*. This lexical-syntactic analysis of the argument structure of the concept core is useful in many ways. First, it helps us identify the position of the defining feature in a precise way. Second, it helps us to decide that an item is a type or extension where semantic and logical analysis mislead us. For example, though a roaster on the surface looks to be a functional type of pan, lexical-syntactic analysis of its gerundive functional feature reveals that it is a quasi type since there is a limited set of central criterial values embedded in the syntactic valency of the gerund. A roaster is a pan used for *roasting* (food). The language puts a selectional restriction constraint on the object of the transitive verb roast since not every type of food can be roast. The limited set of items that fill the object slot causes a roaster to violate the holistic restriction criterion (i.e. the criterion whereby an overspecifying feature of a given conceptual combination can overspecify all the extensions of the same concept, qualifying the combination as a type) that distinguishes types from extensions, since there is no roasting omellette pan, for instance. Thus roaster is a quasi-type and quasi-extension of pan. It is a quasi-type since the overspecifying functional feature failed the holistic restriction test and a quasi-extension since it picks several values of the content CIC (meat, beef . . . etc), not just one of them. Third, we can apply the same analytic technique in the definitional study of abstract concepts. For example, in the definition of medicine as the scientific study of the diseases that afflict body parts, we can observe that the identification criterion *part of the body* occurs as an object of the verb of the relative clause that qualifies the NP *the diseases* in the core feature *study of the diseases*. Using syntactic analysis, we can come up with a clear view of what the concept core, the CIC of any concept are. The concept core is any feature that in and of itself can be a defining feature of the concept that eliminates the need of any other feature. This core can be an abstract functional feature such as the holdability feature in the definition of a cup. It can be an identification criterion such as *body parts* in the definition of medicine or finally it can be an element in the argument structure of a gerundive functional feature, as in the case of one person in the definition of seat.

4:3 A typology of abstract concepts

In this section, I provide a cognitive-semantic taxonomy of abstract concepts which covers six types of concepts: discipline and system concepts, action concepts, attribute concepts, state concepts and entity-related concepts.

4:3:1 Discipline and System concepts

A discipline concept represents a field of knowledge which is concerned with studying a corresponding system concept. This system concept can be an abstract or a concrete system. For example, Medicine, linguistics, science of religion and chemistry are each concerned with a corresponding system concept: body, language, religion and matter respectively. A system concept has a central intensional property and a set of componential properties which constitute the integral parts of which the system is composed. In what follows we analyse four pairs of discipline-system concepts. These pairs are linguistics-language, medicine-body, chemistry-matter and science of religion-religion. The central intensional property of the language system is "a method of communication and/or expression";and the componential properties are such **system components** as syntax, meaning, phonemes and morphemes. These self-same componential properties are the **discipline objects** of linguistics. Each Extension of a discipline concept is related to a componential property of the corresponding system concept. So these componential properties are the central identification criteria whereby extensions of a discipline concept identify themselves as subfields of knowledge focusing on a certain aspect of its corresponding system. Extensions of linguistics are semantics, syntax, morphology and phonology, each of which is concerned with one of the componential properties of the language system: meaning, syntax, morphemes, phonemes and selects it as its discipline object.

The central intensional property of religion can be defined as "a belief in a metaphysical force that controls the world ", and the set of componential properties are the beliefs, rituals, laws and morals the RELIGION system comprises. An Arguably new science of religion is concerned with this system but its extensions (i.e. subfields) have not yet been established by scholastic research.

Chemistry and medicine have concrete concepts as their corresponding system concepts, i.e. matter and human body respectively. The basic intensional property of medicine is a scientific study of diseases that affect the body parts. The identification criterion which relates medicine to its corresponding system concept is *part of the body*. Body parts are thus the componential properties of the body system and the discipline objects of medicine. Each medicine extension corresponds to a single body part so that we have ophthalmology, cardiology, hepatology . . . etc.

The corresponding system concept for chemistry is matter. The basic intensional property of matter is physical substance that has mass and exists as solid or gas or liquid. The basic ingredients of matter that form discrete discipline objects of chemistry are organic compounds that include carbon and inorganic compounds that do not include carbon. It is worthy of notice that the traditional classification of chemistry divides it into five categories: organic chemistry, inorganic chemistry, analytical chemistry, physical chemistry and biochemistry. This classification fails to capture the difference between extensions and types of chemistry. Only organic and inorganic chemistry are extensions of chemistry since they are related to the componential properties of matter, which serve as their identification criteria. Let's take the issue a step further.

4:3:1:1 Types of discipline concepts

A type of a discipline concept is not related to any of the componential properties of its corresponding system concept. It introduces an external element that synthesizes with the discipline concept to form a type. So unlike semantics and morphology, empirical linguistics, statistical linguistics, generative linguistics, philosophical linguistics are all types of linguistics since their overspecifying concepts are not related to a specific componential property of the language system. At the same time, using the holistic overspecification touchstone, we find that the overspecifying concept in each of these types can form a conceptual combination with each extension of linguistics. There is generative semantics, generative morphology and so on. No logical barrier exists that bars the overspecifying concept in types of linguistics from forming a combinational type with each extension of linguistics. Similarly, analytical chemistry, physical chemistry and biochemistry are types of chemistry since they are not focused at a specific component of matter the way organic and inorganic chemistry are. Applying the holistic overspecification test frame used to distinguish types from extensions, we find that analytical organic and analytical inorganic chemistry are a logical possibility and so are physical organic chemistry and bioorganic chemistry, for example. On the other hand, organo-inorganic chemistry is impossible since the discipline objects of organic chemistry and inorganic chemistry are mutually exclusive componential properties of their corresponding system, that is, matter.

In the same way types of medicine are synthetic combinations that are related to the concept as a whole and not to any one of its objects. We have aviation medicine, prophylactic medicine, and critical-case medicine, to mention but a few. It is to be noticed that the peripheral identification criterion introduced by a type of a discipline concept is either an interdisciplinary field or a methodology. Table (5) below summarizes the intensional and componential properties of each of the four discipline concepts cited above, together with their extensions, types and identification criteria.

Concept name	intension	extensions	Corresponding system	types	CIC	Discipline objects	PIC
linguistics	Scientific Study of language	Semantics Syntax Morphology Phonology	language	Psycholinguistics Sociolinguistics	Components of the language system	Meaning Syntax Mrphoemes phonemes	Interdisciplinary field Methodology
chemistry	Scientific Study of matter	Organic chemistry Inorganic chemistry	Matter	Analytic chemistry Physical chemistry Biochemistry	Presence of carbon	Carbon Molecules Non-carbon molecules	Interdisciplinary field Methodology
Science of religion	Scientific Study of religions		Religion		Components of the Religion system	Beliefs, ethics, rituals, laws	
medicine	Scientific study of diseases that affect the body of a living organism	Ophthalmology, Hepatology Cardiology	The body	Aviation medicine Prophylactic medicine Critical-case medicine paediatrics	Body parts	Diseases that Affect parts Of the body	Interdisciplinary field

Table 5: discipline and system concepts

It is to be noticed that when the corresponding system concept of a given discipline concept is a concrete concept, no combination between the latter's extensions is possible since its discipline objects are mutually exclusive components of this system in the real world. On the other hand, when the corresponding system concept of a given discipline concept is an abstract concept, no clear-cut boundaries can be drawn between its extensions. For example, unlike medicine, LINGUISTICS extensions are each concerned with components of a highly abstract system . . . i.e. language and these components are inextricably interrelated. This is the reason why there is morphosemantics, but not ophthalmological dentistry.

4:3:1:2 Extensions and types of system concepts

As has already been pointed out, extensions of system concepts are cognitive instances which either cannot have extensions or have ones that are intransitive in a hierarchy. An example of a non-extensional cognitive instance is any extension of languge, e.g. English, French, Arabic, Cobol, Esperanto . . . etc. British English, American English are types of these languages, not extensions since they are not languages but language varieties. Similarly, shiism and Protestantism are not religions, but religious sects. However, we consider them as extensions of Islam and Christianity respectively since they inherit the basic componential properties of religion. Thus the shiism-islam-religion relationship is an intransitive one, in which shiism is an extension of Islam but not of the superordinate *religion*. In this way it is just like the Big Ben-clock-furniture relationship. Each extension of a system concept does not select a specific criterial value from the intensional or componential properties of the system since these properties are collectively present in the extensions.

Types of system concepts do not introduce an external concept that forms a synthetic conceptual combination. This is because concepts of natural systems represent fixed systems that do not change and do not enter into conceptual combinations in the way discipline concepts do. Types of system concepts are in fact **classificatory labels** of the extensions. These types classify the extensions into sets each of which selects some of the properties of the system concept. For example, the type *natural language* selects from language the natural language extensions which in turn select all the intensional and componential properties of the language system. The type *formal language* subsumes those extensions that represent some category of artificial languages. Extensions belonging under such a category do not pick all the intensional and componential properties of language. For example, mathematical languages and computer languages are used for expression rather than communication. They have syntax but do not have a phonology or morphology and so on. The following two figures show a network representation of the System concept *language* and the discipline concept *linguistics* respectively.

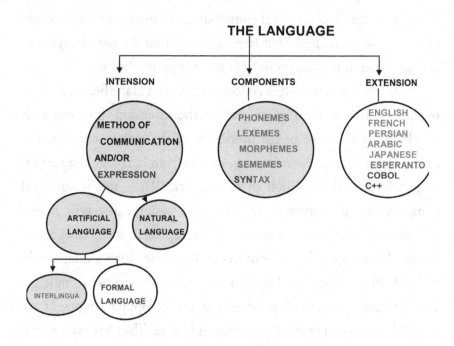

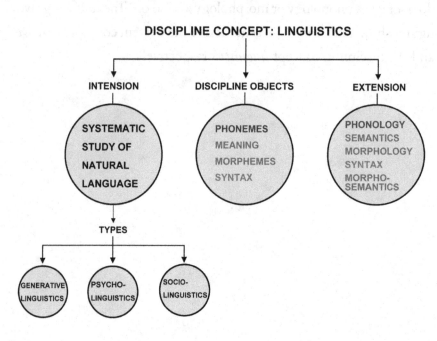

It is clear that the conceptual networks combine the characteristics of the hierarchy and the network. The arrows serve a hierarchical purpose by showing the hierarchical relations between types of the system concept *language*. At the same time these types divide the extensions of the concept language into different sets labeled by the types. The colour scheme serves a networking purpose by linking every extensional set to its pertinent classificatory type and the relevant intensional and componential properties in the language system. The network representing the discipline concept *linguistics* is less complex since each extension maps to a single component of the corresponding system and the types are related to the concept as a whole and not to any specific set of discipline objects and are not therefore classificatory types.

4:3:2 Action concepts

We can apply the conceptual-semantic and conceptual-statistic criteria on action concepts to represent three conceptual modes for actions: extensions, types and the generic concept. The following table shows the extensions and types of two action concepts: hitting and cutting and their identification criteria.

action	CIC	Extension	PIC	Type	Generic equivalent
hitting	instrument	Slapping (hand) Prodding (elbow) Poking (stick) Punching (fist) Slugging (bat) Smacking (palm) Spanking (hand) Whipping (whip) Butting (head) Caning (cane)	Intensity Of action	Peppering Rapping Battering Smiting Tapping Banging Thrashing bashing	Striking Beating

cutting	patient of The cutting action	Clipping (scissors) Haying (grass) Logging (trees) Sawing (saw-wood) Scything (scythe) Shaving (razor-hair) Shearing (shears-foliage) shredding (fabric) Amputating (a limb) Scissoring (scissors) Carving (knife-meat) Beheading (head)	Iterativeness Product shape Purpose	Cropping Hacking Dissecting Truncating Chopping Slicing	Splitting Severing

Table 6: extensions and types of *hitting* and *cutting*

A sample of 20 items has been selected for each of the two concepts. They are related to hitting and cutting by synonymy, hyponomy or troponymy. The analytic central identification criterion for hitting which produces mutually exclusive extensions could be the part of the body which is affected by the hitting action or the instrument used in carrying out this action. A look at the twenty items shows that the instrument criterion is statistically dominant. There is a single synthetic element that represents the peripheral identification criterion, that is the intensity of the hitting act. Thus it is the one that produces the types of hitting as the table shows. To check these findings, we can apply the partial and the holistic overspecification test. By doing this we find that all the types can modify all the extensions and form conceptual combinations with them while the extensions themselves cannot logically form conceptual combinations with each other since their central criterial values are mutually exclusive. Thus we can imagine a banging slap, a banging punch, banging poke or prod, etc. But we cannot conceive of a slapping poke since the instrument used in slapping (i.e. the hand) is mutually exclusive with that used in the act of poking (i.e. a stick). Likewise, we cannot have a *caning butt* or a *punching slap*. Lexical combination between such mutually exclusive extensions could be possible only if the criterial value of the CIC is not in focus. For example, in boxing, there could be a punching prod, i.e. one that is intended to deal a shocking blow to the opponent and not to draw his attention with the elbow. The generic equivalents *beating* and *striking* are deprived of a specific criterial value, central or peripheral. So they are on the same conceptual plane as the generic concept *hitting*. So these are complete synonyms of *hitting* at the generic level.

As for cutting, we can notice from table 6 above two central identification criteria can be valid at the same time for producing mutually exclusive extensions. These are the thing affected by cutting (patient of cutting) or the instrument used in cutting. To solve this problem, we can choose the CIC which is more specific, the one for which there is a single CIC value at a time for each extension. For example, in the case of beheading, the head is more specifically in focus than the sword or any other sharp tool used in carrying out the beheading action. In other words, there is no specific tool that is solely used for this purpose, but there is inevitably one and only one specific thing that is affected by this act, that is the head. In the case of scything, however, the instrument is the specific element, not the patient of cutting. There are five cutting extensions out of twelve in which the patient of cutting is purely more specific than the instrument (haying-logging-shredding-amputating-beheading) and four ones in which the patient and instrument are equally specific (sawing-shaving-shearing-carving) and three in which the instrument is more specific (clipping-scything-scissoring). So we use the *patient of cutting* as the central identification criterion since it is statistically dominant. There are other peripheral identification criteria that determine the types. They are those of purpose (dissecting, i.e. cutting for the purpose of examining), iterativeness (chopping, hacking, cropping) and product shape (truncating, slicing). These types have no specific criterial values, either instrument or specific cutting patient, other than these peripheral values. By applying the holistic overspecification test to the types we find that all of them can logically (though not necessarily lexically) enter into conceptual combinations with the extensions. Items devoid of central or peripheral values are synonyms of the generic concept, that is, they are generic equivalents.

4:3:3 Attribute concepts

An attribute concept is an abstract concept which represents an inherent quality in a thing or person. It can be a physical trait like tallness and shortness, a moral attribute such as bravery or cowardice. It can be a mental quality such as intelligence and astuteness.

We can arrive at the central identification criterion and the peripheral identification criterion of attribute concepts by analyzing the conceptual nouns representing them in the electronic Wordnet database. A subcategory of attribute nouns in this lexical database is that of mental faculty nouns. The analysis shows that the central IC in mental attribute concepts is the specific mental faculty the mental attribute concept represents. Five faculties can be detected: perception, imagination, attention, memory, judgement, sensibility and intuition. These are the central criteria that identify the extensions of the concept *mental attribute*. Types are determined by the domains in which these faculties are applied. For example, the judgment faculty is applied to the aesthetic, legal and linguistic domains so that we have legal judgment, aesthetic judgement . . . etc. as shown in table 7

Faculty	extensions	types
Perception	perceptiveness	Cognitive perceptiveness
Judgement	Judiciousness, Perspicaciousness Discreteness, Discrimination, Finesse Grumption, Sagacity	Legal judgment, aesthetic Judgement Musicianship
Attention	Attentiveness, Vigilance, Concentration, Intentness, Sense of purpose, Will power	
Thinking	Contemplativeness, Deliberateness Introspectiveness, Profoundness	Critical thinking
Intuition	Foresight, insight, prevision, Clairvoyance, Discernment	Scientific intuition
Intelligence	Brilliance, Ingeniousness, Quickwittedness, quickness	Artificial intelligence
Imagination	Imaginativeness, creativity	Artistic imagination, poetic imagination
Sensibility	Logicality, rationality	
Skill	Acuity, Acumen, Adroitness, Cleverness, Advertence Aptness, Artfulness, Astuteness, Versatility	Showmanship Telekinesis
Memory	Recall Recollection Retention	Short-term memory

Table 7: *mental attribute*: types and extensions

This is congruent with recent views in faculty psychology. Traditional views in faculty psychology hold that each faculty is horizontal rather than functional. This means that there is, for instance, one judgment faculty for all content domains. So there is no exclusive module for musical appreciation, for example. The functional view holds that there is an independent functional module for every discrete domain which is a combination of the given faculty and the domain content. According to this model, there is a module for aesthetic judgment and another autonomous one for legal judgment and so on. The modularity hypothesis postulates that mental faculties are both horizontal and functional[133]. Each faculty is shared horizontally between the domain modules. Thus in our present model, the extensions represent the horizontal faculties while the types represent faculty-independent content domains. It is important to note that the extensions listed for each faculty are mostly synonyms of the same extension since they do not pick different criterial values but are related to one criterion, that is the given faculty. For example, attentiveness, vigilance and concentration share the same core faculty of attention without overpecifying it with a criterial value of their own. So they are synonymous extensions rather than different ones while will power and sense of purpose overspecify the attentiveness faculty by an analytic cognitive element, that is *will power*. By applying the holistic and partial overspecification test frame, we find that there is a high possibility of conceptual combination between extensions related to different faculties. For example, we can envisage logical discernment and creative quickwittedness. This is due to the interdependence between the faculty modules in the mind. The overspecifying domain-specific concept in each type can overspecify each extension of mental attribute regardless of the specific faculty to which the extension is related. We can have aesthetic discrimination, aesthetic foresight, aesthetic adroitness, and aesthetic creativity and so on.

4:3:4 State concepts

We can argue that lack of a positive mental attribute leads to a related negative state. We can think of the extensions of a certain category of mental states as a result of temporary absence of an attribute. For example there are three attributes the absence of which can lead to three corresponding negative states whose extensions and types are listed below. These attributes are imagination, attention and memory. The absence of imagination leads to a state of illusion, that of attentiveness leads to a state of absent-mindedness while the loss of memory causes a state of amnesia.

state	extensions	Types
Illusion	Hallucination, reverie, make-believe, fanciness	
Absent-mindedness	Abstractedness, distraction,	
Amnesia	Anterograde Amnesia, retrograde amnesia, prosopamnesia	Traumatic amnesia,

Table 8: mental state

Extensions of Amnesia are related to memory-specific criteria such as the range of time covered and the object of memory loss. Anterograde and retrograde Amnesia are related to the temporal criterion while prosopamnesia is related to the forgotten object criterion as it means a loss of the ability to remember faces. Traumatic amnesia introduces an external element related to the aetiology of the syndrome rather than to the core of amnesia. So traumatic Amnesia is a type.

4:3:5 Entity-related concepts

An entity-related concept is a concept that has no physical realization in a conceptual noun but which is lexically realized in an entitive noun only. Examples are the concepts *job, idea, price, craft* ... Etc. Thus any entitive noun that has no CN counterpart is a lexical realization of this type of concepts. They don't have a semantic taxonomy of their own but can be taxonomized by themes. So an economic entitive concept group includes such items as price, fee, and tax. A mental entitive concept group includes such items as notion, idea and attitude. Following the usual methodologies we have been using so far, we can analyze two examples of these concepts in the manner shown in table 9

Concept name	intension	CIC	extensions	PIC	types	Generic Equivalent
Price	Amount of money offered Or asked when sth Is bought or sold	A specific thing For which money is Charged or offered	Agio Admission, entrance money, carfare, corkage, docking, handling charge, lighterage, portage, service charge, subway fare, return fare, toll wharfage	Rate whereby price Is determined	cost price selling price unit price upset price cut price half price	
Job	A regular activity that One does for pay	A specific regular activity	Accountancy, engineering, Mechanics, banking, carpentry, cartography, farming, dressmaking, Journalism, gardening, Librarianship, marketing, midwifery, plumbery, teaching, Trucking, woodcraft, drafting, public relations, book-binding, animal-husbandry, House-painting, landscape gardening, stockbrokerage.	Time scale Skill-level	Part-time job Full-time job Learned profession	Profession, vocation, career.

Table 9: conceptual-semantic analysis of entity-related concepts

Table 9 above shows the 17 price items found in Wordnet. They are divided into extensions and types according to their central and peripheral identification criteria as shown in the table. The 27 job items represent a sample taken from some 200 job items found in Wordnet dictionary. Their extensions and types as well as their intensional properties are determined by semantic analysis which reveals the CIC and PIC of the concept job as table 9 illustrates.

Chapter 5

Mental processing of abstract nouns

5:1 Theoretical framework

S everal theoretical approaches have been incorporated into the theoretical framework of the current study to achieve four purposes. The first purpose is to establish an analogy between concrete concepts and abstract concepts in terms of internal structure and inter-conceptual relations. To achieve this purpose, two basic classical view assumptions have been adopted, that is the summary representation assumption and the nesting assumption. By virtue of the summary representation principle, we could proceed from the imperceptual features of object concepts to the non-perceptual ones of abstract concepts. We also reconciled the summary representation assumption of the classical view with that of the exemplar view so as to establish an analogy between the extensions of abstract concepts and those of concrete concepts. According to this reconciliation, a concept is a summary representation both of an entire class and an individual instance. The probabilistic view is also integrated into this theoretical framework as a statistical technique for selecting the highly-weighted semantic elements as a basis for pre-empirical semantic analysis. This theoretical hybridization has important methodological implications for the pre-processing procedures of semantic analysis which we believe should precede any psychological experiments.

The classical view's nesting assumption has been adopted together with two main theories in semantics and propositional logic, that is, the theory of extensionalism and *possible worlds semantics*. The nesting assumption was particularly useful in finding a parallel between the domain of concrete concepts and that of abstract concepts with regard to the property inheritance and transitivity principles. The other two theories are crucial in establishing the analogy between the outside world and the inner world of cognition.

The second purpose is to set up a method for analyzing the intensional properties of concepts with a view to transforming this method into a technique for defining abstract concepts. To achieve this aim, charges against the classical view's assumption of defining features had to be answered in order to build a solid definitional theory for abstract concepts. The assumption is that if a definitional theory of concepts should fail on the cognitive level, we can use it at least as a metacognitive technique for defining and analyzing the internal content of a concept. The third purpose is related to investigating the lexical processing of abstract concepts in the bilingual mind. We propose to access the bilingual mind through accessing the monolingual mind of each of the two languages mastered by the bilingual translator. This means that we have to conduct tests on monolingual Arabic and English subjects as well as bilingual translators. The tests conducted with the first two groups of subjects involve item production tasks (see below). The kind of tests conducted with bilinguals are RT tests involving translation of contextualized and decontextualized conceptual nouns in a manner explained in detail in this chapter.

By comparing results of monolingual and bilingual tests, it is hoped that we can lay our hands on some universal principles underlying conceptual transfer between the two languages. The fourth purpose is the investigation of lexical production of abstract nouns in actual translated texts. The aim here is to see the impact of the process on the product. For example, given that extensions take less processing in the mind of translators than types, does it follow that nominal realizations of extensions are in some cases preferred to those of types where a choice between the two is open to the translator? To answer such a question we need to develop a cognitive approach to semantic relations and then apply it in our analysis of translational equivalents of abstract nouns in the target language. This is the task we undertake in section 5-3 of this chapter.

5:1:1 Processing hypotheses

Two major types of processing hypotheses are subject to empirical testing in this chapter. There are two bilingual hypotheses based on a major monolingual hypothesis.

5:1:1:1 The monolingual hypothesis

In an item production task, it is hypothesized that extensions, being analytically embedded in the concept, are produced more frequently than types, which are synthetic combinations that entail the introduction of an external element. This hypothesis will be checked both with English and Arabic native speakers. Typicality ratings will be performed on those items which have been actually produced by subjects in both languages rather than those which have not. It is assumed that the more typical items will mostly be the ones frequently listed by subjects in the item production tasks.

5:1:1:2 Bilingual hypotheses

In actual translation, lexical transfer of analytical combinations, i.e. extensions is supposed to take less processing and therefore less time than that of synthetic combinations since the former are already embedded in the concept and thus the overhead of processing an external synthetic element is saved.

It is assumed that the typicality ratings of the items produced by monolingual users of the source language and the target language separately will be correlated with the processing results of lexical transfer of abstract nouns by bilingual translators. Items that take less processing in lexical transfer are expected to be themselves the ones calculated by typicality ratings.

5:2 Methodological issues

Having segregated items into types and extensions, the cognitive semanticist will need to verify the psychological validity of his analysis by asking subjects to perform standard perceptual and semantic tasks similar to those conducted by empirical concept psychologists. For example, he can ask subjects to produce category members, given category names (Batting and Montague, 1967). He can analyze the data he elicits from subjects to see whether subjects mostly produce analytic items or synthetic ones, that is whether the analytic extensions or the synthetic types are more readily produced as category members.

Guided by literature on the psychology of concepts and our differentiation between semantic identification and perceptual identification, we can classify category membership tasks into three classes: Perceptual tasks, perceptual-semantic tasks and semantic tasks. In a purely perceptual task, subjects are presented with pictures of probes and are asked to assign a probe to a target, which is the name of the superordinate concept. In a perceptual-semantic task subjects are asked to categorize items based on perceptual features stored in their memories. Each subject is given a category name and is then presented with names of individual items to judge whether an item belongs to the category. Thus he is presented with probes and targets only as names. In this process, a subject mentally compares the perceptual features of both the target and the probe in his memory as they are triggered by the printed words. In a purely semantic task, each individual is presented with a category name and is asked to produce as many members as he can of that category from memory. Or he can be given some items and is then required to name the superordinate category. In such tasks, a subject is not supposed to compare features of two concepts, the subordinate and the superordinate since he is not in a situation where the two are directly placed opposite to each other, ready for comparison. What he actually does is a lexical-semantic work which involves retrieving from memory the hyponyms or the hypernyms of targets and probes.

Clearly, semantic tasks are the ones most suitable for categorizing abstract concepts. We will use them to test our monolingual processing hypothesis concerning the categorization of such concepts.

In verifying the second processing hypothesis we resort to the RT technique which involves measuring the response times Arab translators take in the lexical transfer of abstract nouns from English into Arabic. In order to corroborate the third processing hypothesis regarding the correlation between the typicality of abstract concepts and the amount of processing required in translating these concepts from English into Arabic, we need first to measure this typicality by using one of the standard methods followed in calculating the typicality rates of concrete concepts.

By comparing the typicality effects based on responses made by native speakers of each language separately with the results of the bilingual processing task undertaken by translators, we can hope to find common semantic principles across languages.

5:3 Monolingual Processing by SL and TL speakers

In our initial monolingual hypothesis, it was postulated that in an item production task, extensions, being analytically embedded in the concept, are produced more frequently than types, which are synthetic combinations that entail the introduction of an external element. To verify this hypothesis, an item production task was assigned to a sample of 20 Arabic native speakers and another sample of 20 English native speakers. Six categories of abstract concepts were selected for item production by the native speakers of both languages: science, literature, art, language, religion and law.

5:3:1 Pre-processing task

Following the methodology established in 5-2, semantic analysis has to precede any psychological task so as to be able to detect the relation between the semantic content of lexical items and our metacognitive intuitions about concepts. Such intuitions can be gleaned from subject responses in item production tasks. Following the normal method we have used so far, table 10 below shows a dissection of the six categories in terms of their intensional properties, identification criteria and extensional range. A random sample of several lexical items was selected for each category in both languages from the Wordnet English dictionary and an electronic monolingual Arabic lexicon.

superordinate	intension	CIC	extensions	PIC	Types
Science علم	Systematic Investigation, Description, explanation Of phenomena through Observation and experimentation	Systematic study of phenomena	Biology, Chemistry Physics Psychology Sociology فيزياء كيمياء أحياء رياضيات علم نفس	Method: Observation, experimentation	Empirical science Experimental Science علم تجريبي علم إمبريقي
Literature الأدب	The art of Written works Pertaining to a given period, language or culture	An art of written forms	Novel-Poetry Essay-Drama قصة شعر مقال مقامات مسرح	Period Culture Literary tradition	Epic literature Roman Literature Victorian literature أدب عربي أدب فارسي

Art الفن	a diverse range of human activities, creations, and modes of expression that involve deliberate arrangement of symbols to influence the senses, emotions and intellect	A range of creative activities (forms)	Drawing Painting Sculpture Dancing رسم نحت تمثيل معمار	Style-Genre-Era-Medium	Abstract art Expressionist art Plastic arts Performing arts Decorative arts فن تجريدي فنون تطبيقية فن تشكيلي
Language اللغة	a method of communication and/or expression that involves a system of elements including syntax, phonemes, meaning and morphemes	a system of elements including syntax, phone-mes, meaning and morphemes	English Arabic Esperanto Cobol إنجليزية عربية إسبيرانتو باسكال	Mode of communication	Formal Natural Artificial Interlingua لغات طبيعية لغة اصطناعية لغة وسيطة
Religion الدين	A system of beliefs, rituals, laws and morals that overlies a belief in a metaphysical Force that controls the world	A system of beliefs, rituals, laws and morals	Islam Christianity Hinduism الإسلام المسيحية اليهودية الهندوسية	Mode of faith	Divine Non-divine دين سماوي دين غير سماوي
القانون	A system of rules and regulations established in a community by some authority and applicable to its people within a given domain	A system of rules and regulations	constitutional law. Statutory Law القــانون الدستوري قانون العقوبات	Domain	Labour law-Business law-Family law Traffic law قانون العمل قانون الأسرة قانون المرور

Table 10: conceptual-semantic analysis of six superordinate categories

As the table 10 shows, extensions of non-system categories, i.e. science, art and literature each represents a variable in the central identification criterion which is part of the definition of the concept. For example, extensions of science are such variables of "the systematic study of phenomena" as biology, psychology, sociology . . . etc. The central identification criterion is "the phenomenon being studied", which is replaced by a specific phenomenon inherent in each extension of science. Similarly, the written forms in the definition of literature are variables represented by each individual extension of literature, e.g. novel, poetry . . . etc. In the case of the three system categories, i.e. language, religion and law, the extensions are whole subsystems each of which does not represent a specific variable in the range of the CIC of the superordinate but rather inherits a set of elements. For example, primitive religions do not have all the elements of such full-fledged religions as Abrahamic religions. They have a ritual system, but not a system of theological creeds like that found in Christianity or a legal system such as the one found in Islam. One can argue for drawing a distinction between natural systems and artificial systems. A natural system originates and develops in the natural course of events while an artificial system is deliberately man-made. Language and religion can serve as examples of natural systems while law is an artificial system. Extensions of natural systems are cognitive instances while those of artificial systems are mentally-constructed subsystems. In non-system categories, a type represents an external element related to a peripheral identification criterion which may or may not be explicit in the category's definition. As I have indicated before, sometimes a type does not represent an external element but simply serves a distributory and a regrouping function, that is, it distributes the componential properties of the category among the extensions and thereby regroups them into sets bearing the label of the type. This is particularly true of natural system categories. For example, formal language restricts certain properties of language to certain extensions. Unlike natural languages, formal languages have a syntax and meaning but they don't have phonemes or morphemes and are used for one-way communication to express matters of fact and not for two-way interaction.

5:3:2 Experiment 1: item production tasks

5:3:2:1 Stimulants

Stimulants in the item production task are the six categories mentioned above. Category names were presented to subjects in tables. Subjects were asked to produce at least five items for each category. The categories selected are superordinate categories, not generic (middle-level) ones. This is because middle-level categories such as chemistry, physics, dancing . . . etc require some sort of specialized technical knowledge. The aim of the task is not to test any technical knowledge about concepts but to know whether subjects produce analytic concepts (extensions) as items belonging under a specific category or synthetic ones (types).

Participants

Subjects participating in the English item production task are 20 English native speakers and those participating in the Arabic item production task are 20 Arabic native speakers. Native speakers in both tasks are university graduates or undergraduates and were chosen so as to represent different educational backgrounds.

Their ages ranged from 20 to 35 so as to insure a homogeneous memory status. It is worthy of notice that the 20 participants in each monolingual task are only the ones who could understand the instructions that were supplied on the table sheet. Those who failed to comply with the instructions, as evidenced by their performance, were eliminated. So the number of candidates who successfully participated in the Arabic item production task was 20 out of 50 potential candidates and the number of actual participants in the English item production task was 20 out of 70 potential candidates.

Procedure

As mentioned above, each subject in both item production tasks was presented with six categories and asked to produce at least five items for each category. An item was defined for the subjects as a family member of the category or simply a subcategory. Illustrations were given from concrete concepts so that subjects could use the analogy to produce items of abstract concept categories. In the instructions sheet, subjects were cautioned against producing false items such as domain words. Domain words are words thematically related to a category but do not represent an item of this category. For example, Albert Einstein and space were produced as items of science by some subjects. A process of sorting out was carried out to sieve off the real items from false items. A true item was ticked (√) on the table and was only considered in the sequential order of the five items while false items were ignored. Subjects who produced more false items than the required minimum of 5 true items of the category were naturally eliminated from the list of actual participants.

Discussion and results

With the exception of the concept Law, the number of extensions listed as items for each of the six categories far exceeded the number of types in both the English and the Arabic item production tasks. Tables 11, 12 show the final statistics extracted from both tasks.

superordinate	Number of extensions	Number of types	Total	Most typical Item
science	97	3	100	Biology
literature	79	21	100	Poetry
art	86	14	100	Dancing, drawing
language	93	7	100	English
religion	89	11	100	Islam
law	15	85	100	International law

Table 11: English item production task

superordinate	Number of extensions	Number of types	Total	Most typical Item
علم	100	0	100	أحياء
أدب	73	27	100	قصة
فن	96	4	100	رسم
لغة	99	1	100	العربية
الدين	98	2	100	الإسلام
قانون	21	79	100	جنائي

Table 12: Arabic item production task

It is to be noticed that the number of extensions and types listed by English and Arabic subjects in both monolingual tasks are almost identical with a slight increase in the number of types in the English task. Law is an exception in both tasks. In both, the number of Law types far exceeds the number of its extensions by almost the same margin. This can be explained by arguing that the CIC of the artificial system Law is related to rules and regulations, which requires a sophisticated knowledge of the law beyond the reach of non-law experts. Types, on the contrary, are related to domains in which the law is applied and these domains are part of everyday knowledge since they represent extra-legal facets of life to which law is put to use. This is why native speakers of both languages listed more types of law than extensions.

It is worthy of notice that pre-processing semantic analysis of the six categories proved to be consistent with the data provided by the English and Arabic native speakers in the two item production tasks. The items supplied by participants in both tasks reflect the identification criteria, central and peripheral, used in identifying extensions and types, as has been demonstrated in the pre-processing semantic analysis stage. Tables 13, 14 give a 10-percent sample of the 100 items listed for each of the six categories by subjects in both tasks.

superordinate	item	classification	
science	Physical science-Experimental science	Ext	type
			√
	Forensic science-psychology-chemistry-Biology-Physics-ornithology-histology-astronomy	√	
Literature	English literature Classical literature		√
	Novel-poetry-old Poetry-story-short story-Islamic story-drama-magazine writing	√	

Art	Modern art impressionistic art		√
	Drawing, painting, Oil painting, music, singing, dancing, canvas, Acting.	√	
language	Agglutinative language Indo-European language		√
	Arabic, English, French, Italian, Turkish, Albanian, Dutch, German	√	
Religion	Polytheistic Monotheistic		√
	Islam, Christianity, Hinduism, Buddhism Judaism, Magus, Protestantism, sunnism	√	
Law	National law, Environment law, Woman law, civil law, international law, child law, human rights law		√
	Constitutional law, regulatory law	√	

Table 13: a sample of the 100 items listed for each category by subjects in The English item production task.

superordinate	item	classification	
		Ext	type
علم	فيزياء،كيمياء،أحياء،رياضــيات ، إحــصاء،تاريخ،علم الــنفس، علــم الاجتماع،جيولوجي،هندسة	√	
أدب	أدب حديث، أدب معاصر		√
	شعر،كتابة،نثر،قصة قصيرة،رواية ،مقال،رحلات،مسرح	√	
فن	فن تجريدي فن كلاسيكي		√
	تمثيــل، نحــت، تــصوير، رسم،رقص،موسيقى، الخط،الطباعة	√	
اللغة	سامية		√
	إنجليزيــة، فرنــسية، عبريــة، ألمانية،أســـبانية،أردية، أرامية،إيطالية،برتغالية	√	
الدين	سماوي، غير سماوي		√
	الإســلام، المــسيحية، اليهوديــة، البوذية،الهندوسية،الماجوسية، الزرادشتية، المزدكية	√	

القانون	جنائي،مـــــــــدني،تجاري،قانون العمـــل،الأحوال الشخــصية،الأسرة والطفل،دولي،قانون المرافعات		√
	القانون الدستوري،قانون العقوبات	√	

Table 14 a sample of the 100 items listed for each category by subjects in the Arabic item production task

The sample shows the proportionate distribution of extensions and types. A comparison of this sample with table 10 reveals how identical the sample tables are with the pre-processing table in terms of the ICs and their relevant types and extensions. For example, both in the lexical pre-processing sample and the item production ones, the PICs of period and genre are the overspecifying concepts of items identified as types of art and literature, as in *classical literature* and *abstract art*. This applies equally well to English and Arabic.

5:3:2:1 Typicality effects

Typicality effects in both tasks were calculated on the basis of the combination of two factors: the number of times an item is listed as the first item for a given category and the total frequency of the item. For example, In the English task, drawing was listed as an item of art 11 times, six times out of which it ranked as the first item. Thus its typicality score= total frequency + frequency as first item. Therefore, the TS of drawing =11+6=17. It is the most typical art item. In both English and Arabic tasks, biology, drawing and Islam are the most typical items of science, art and religion respectively. Typicality effects are correlated with item production results in both tasks since the most typical items are the ones with high production frequency, i.e. extensions in five categories and types in law. This proves our initial monolingual hypothesis that extensions have a higher production frequency than types in an item production task and that extensions rather than types are the most typical items.

5:3:3 Experiment 2: Bilingual processing by English-Arabic translators.

The basic bilingual hypothesis postulates that in actual translation, lexical transfer of analytical combinations, i.e. extensions is supposed to take less processing and therefore less time than that of synthetic combinations since the former are already embedded in the concept and thus the overhead of processing an external synthetic element is saved In verification of this bilingual hypothesis, an empirical test was designed to measure the processing overhead required to transfer concepts from English into Arabic. The aim is to discover the difference in processing time taken in the translation of superordinates, their types and extensions. For this end, a group of 20 translators were presented with names of nine categories, and asked to translate them from English into Arabic. The response time measured in milliseconds reflects the targeted difference in processing time.

Stimulants

The stimulants are names of nine categories administered as decontextualized individual items and as words-in-context. They are divided into three sets. Each set comprises a category name, an extension and a type as follows:

superordinate	science	Language	Hitting
Type	Experimental science	Natural language	Battering
Extension	physics	French	slapping

Table 15: nine category names in the bilingual task

It is obvious that the *science* set includes discipline concepts and the *language* set represents a system concept while the *hitting* set includes three modes of the action concept *hitting*: The concept name itself (superordinate), a type of hitting (battering) and an extension of it (slapping). The 20 translators participating in the experiment were divided into two groups each including 10 translators. Group A were asked to translate the category names as decontextualized words and Group B were presented with sentences each including a category name and asked to translate it based on the context. The sentences are taken from natural texts on the internet. They are divided into three sets each covering three category modes.

Set 1

A) This is a test to assess your level of LANGUAGE awareness.
B) We must assess the state of our knowledge of NATURAL LANGUAGE.
C) We have to evaluate the degree of our knowledge of FRENCH.

Set 2

A) HITTING your wife is against the law.
B) BATTERING your wife is a crime.
C) SLAPPING your daughter is a gross crime.

Set 3

A) The one suggests that SCIENCE can exact remarkable changes.

B) The third argues that EXPERIMENTAL SCIENCE can come up with new discoveries.

C) The second maintains that PHYSICS can bring about fresh innovations.

Participants

Participants in the two groups mentioned are professional translators at an age ranging from 25 to 35.

Procedure

In the decontextualized part of the experiment, each member of group A was handed nine cards each with one category name written on it. Each subject was instructed to keep the cards face down and to pick them up one by one when instructed. Once asked, each subject picked a card and translated the category name aloud. The response time was measured from the moment he/she started looking at the category name till the moment he/she uttered the translation. After the response time was recorded, the subject was asked to write down the translation on the card. In the contextualized part of the experiment, each member in group B was handed nine cards on each of which was written one of the nine stimulant sentences. In each sentence, the category name was highlighted in yellow. Each was asked to read the sentence silently and then say his/her translation of the category name aloud. The response time was measured from the moment the translator started looking at the sentence till the moment he/she uttered the translation. After the response time was recorded, each subject was asked to write down the translation of the contextualized category name on the card

Results and discussion

The decontextualized test:

Table 16 shows the response times in milliseconds which were recorded for the ten subjects of group A in the decontextualized test.

category	S1	S2	S3	S4	S5	S6	S7	S8	S9	S10
science	2.9	2.0	2.3	3.1	3, 2	2.6	1.2	2.5	2.5	3.4
experimental science	3.9	3.9	3.9	4.2	4, 1	3, 9	2	3.0	2.9	5.0
physics	3.5	3.1	4.4	2.8	2, 7	2, 6	1, 9	2.3	2.6	4.1
language	3.9	2.3	2.4	1, 8	3	0.7	1, 4	1.8	2.1	2.8
Natural language	7.2	4.5	3.4	5, 3	3, 3	2.4	2, 8	4.6	2.5	4.0
French	3.5	2.1	2.0	3, 3	3.5	2, 6	2, 4	3.4	2.0	3.0
hitting	3.1	1.9	2.0	5.1	3, 1	3.6	1, 6	2.4	2.3	2.6
battering	5.3	3.5	3.7	5	5, 3	4.9	4.3	3.1	3.1	3.9
slapping	8.7	3.9	4.8	4.4	3, 1	2, 5	1.7	2.5	2.9	3.5

Table 16: RTs in milliseconds recorded for group A in the decontextualized test.

A quick glance at the above table reveals that the response times for types are more than those recorded for extensions and superordinates. To obtain accurate statistics, we can resort to the mean as a data summarization tool. The mean response time for each category mode (superordinate-extension-type) can be obtained by adding the RTs for each category mode and dividing the sum by the total number of scores for this mode. The total number of scores for each of the three category modes is 30.

So the mean RT= sum of the RT scores÷total number of scores.

Superordinate mean RT

Sum of the Superordinate scores = science Rt scores+Language Rt scores+hitting Rt scores =
2.9+2+2.3+3.1+3.2+2.6+1.2+2.5+2.5+3.4+3.9+2.3+2.4+1.8+3+0.7+1.4+1.8+2.1+2.8+3.1+1.9+2+5.1+3.1+3.6+1.6+2.4+2.3+2.6=75.6

Mean= 75.6÷30=2.52

Mean RT for types

Sum of the Type scores=experimental science scores+natural language scores+battering scores=
3.9+3.9+3.9+4.2+4.1+3.9+2+3+2.9+5+7.2+4.5+3.4+5.3+3.3+2.4+2.8+4.6+2.5+4+5.3+3.5+3.7+5+5.3+4.9+4.3+3.1+3.1+3.9=118.3

Mean=118.3÷30=3.96 =4

Mean RT for extensions:

Sum of Extension scores = Physics scores+French scores+slapping scores=
3.5+3.1+4.4+2.8+2.7+2.6+1.9+2.3+2.6+4.1+3.5+2.1+2+3.3+3.5+2.6+2.4+3.4+2+3+8.7+3.9+4.8+4.4+3.1+2.5+1.7+2.5+29+3.5=95.8

Mean= 95.8÷30=3.19=3

The mean RT of types across the three sets is 4, which is bigger than both the mean RT of extensions and that of the superordinates. We can predict from these results that the conceptual transfer of decontexualized nominal items can be consistent with the hypothesis that synthetic concepts (types) require more processing than that required by superordinates and analytic concepts (extensions) in the bilingual mind of English-Arabic translators.

The contextualized test:

Table 17 shows the response times in milliseconds which were recorded for the ten subjects of group B in the contextualized test.

category	S1	S2	S3	S4	S5	S6	S7	S8	S9	S10
science	6.9	5.5	13.4	7.4	6.5	23.2	7.6	4.8	5.5	10
experimental science	6.5	5.3	10.1	16	6.3	8.2	8.3	6.2	5.0	9.4
physics	9.2	2.6	6.1	10.6	7.1	6.5	8.0	5.3	4.8	9
language	8.2	3.1	9.2	6.3	7.1	13.5	7.9	5.2	5.8	9.3
Natural language	7.5	3.8	9	7.2	6.9	9.7	11.6	5.7	8.9	10
French	5.8	3.1	5.5	14.5	2.8	5.5	6.3	4.9	5.4	8.5
Hitting	4.1	8.3	3.8	6.4	5.5	3.9	5.9	5.2	4.9	8.4
Battering	7.6	9.3	4	14.3	6.7	8.7	10.7	6.9	6.1	8.4
Slapping	5.4	3.9	3.2	6.7	3.8	5.5	5.5	6.0	5.9	8.6

Table 17: RTs in milliseconds recorded for group B in the contextualized test

We can calculate the mean response time for the superordinates, types and extensions in the same way it was calculated for the decontexualized test results. The total number of RTs scored by the ten subjects in Group B for each category mode is 30 so that:

The Superordinate mean RT=

Sum of the Superordinate scores ÷ 30

Sum of the Superordinate scores = science Rt scores+Language Rt scores+hitting Rt scores =

6.9+5.5+13.4+7.4+6.5+23.2+7.6+4.8+5.5+10+8.2+3.1+9.2+6.3+7.1+13.5 +7.9+5.2+5.8+9.3+4.1+8.3+3.8+6.4+5.5+3.9+5.94+5.2+4.9+8.4=219

Mean=219÷30=7.3

Type mean RT=

Sum of type scores ÷30

Sum of the Type scores=experimental science scores+natural language scores+battering scores=

6.5+5.3+10.1+16+6.3+8.2+8.3+6.2+5+9.4+7.5+3.8+9+7.2+6.9+9.7+11.6 +5.7+8.9+10+7.6+9.3+4+14.3+6.7+8.7+10.7+6.9+6.1+8.4=244, 4

Mean=244.4÷30=8.14

Extension mean RT=

Sum of extension scores÷30

Sum of Extension scores = Physics scores+French scores+slapping scores=

9.2+2.6+6.1+10.6+7.1+6.5+8+5.3+4.8+9+5.8+3.1+5.5+14.5+2.8+5.5+6.3 +4.9+5.4+8.5+5.4+3.9+3.2+6.7+3.8+5.5+5.5+6+5.9+8.6=186

Mean=186÷30=6.2

The mean response time for types, as the above statistics show, is higher than that of extensions and superordinates. This result is consistent with that of the decontextualized test and lends credence to the basic bilingual hypothesis which predicts that response times for types will be higher than those scored for extensions and superordinates. We can generalize by predicting that in a larger population, this result holds true whether the lexical items encapsulating the concepts are contextualized or decontextualized. It is to be observed that the mean response times for all the three category modes are higher in the contextualized test results than those of the decontexualized test results encountered above. This can be attributed to the contextual noise resulting from the overhead of processing a whole sentence. It is clear from the autonomous model exhibited by the monolingual task results and shared model exhibited by the bilingual task results that analytic concepts are given processing priority in the bilingual mind of translators over synthetic ones.

Chapter 6

Lexical Transfer of Abstract Nouns in Bilingual Texts

This chapter deals with lexical transfer of abstract nouns in English-Arabic translation. It discusses how the interplay between the text and the translator's interpretive mind can affect the conceptual make-up of the source language lexical items when they are translated into the target language. Section 6-1 provides an account of the characteristics and constraints of entitive nouns and conceptual nouns in Arabic. Section 6-2 provides a thorough analysis of six abstract noun categories and their translational equivalents in a bilingual corpus.

6.1 Conceptual nouns and Entitive nouns in Arabic

In chapter three (4.1.3.1), we laid down some semantic and syntactic rules for the identification of conceptual nouns and entitive nouns in English. In the light of these criteria, we set about the task of laying down similar rules for the identification of CNs and ENs in Arabic, bearing in mind the syntactic and case-specific differences between the two languages.

A Conceptual noun (CN) in Arabic has the following characteristics:

1) it is uncountable
2) it is generic in scope, i.e. it refers to a general truth rather than a specific entity. For example, in 1 below:
   1) Altamyyz ʔala asas aldyn waa alʔyrq walwMa marfwd̲ (discrimination on the basis of religion, language or race is unacceptable) aldyn (religion) refers to all religions, not to a specific religion.
3) it is able to introduce a general statement, in which case it must be prefixed by the definite article AL A general statement in Arabic is a nominal sentence which consists of an initial nominal (mubtada) and a nominal or verbal phrase predicate (Khabar). The predicate expresses a general fact or truth about the initial nominal as in 2 below
   2) *Alʔilm nwron* (literally: Knowledge is illumination).

In this case a CN cannot be assigned a nunnation case diacritic.

When a CN does not introduce a general statement, it can be definite or indefinite as in 3a and 3b below:

> *3a) Öh̲ibo almaaʔrifaa* (I love knowledge)
> *3b) HaaÖa alamro la yah̲tajo ila maaʔrifaatin* (This matter does not require knowledge)

In 3b the CN *"maaʔrefaatin"* is assigned a case ending diacritic.

An Entitive noun (EN) in Arabic must have the following constraints:

1) It cannot introduce a general statement as is clear in 3a and b below

4a) *Fikraaton amron jaayid* ** (Idea is good)

4b) *Fikraaton xaataaraat ly bilamsi* (An idea came to me yesterday)

4a is ungrammatical and 3b) is not a general statement, since the predicate does not convey a general truth about the subject. Thus fekra is an entitive noun

   2) It must have a specific scope of reference, as 4a and 4b illustrate

      5a *HaaÒihi fikraaton haasaanaa* (this is a good idea)

      5b *ʔilm la yaanfaaʔ* (a knowledge to no good)

In 5a it is clear that *Fekraton* refers to a specific idea. In 5b, the noun *ʔilm*on is an anaphoric, particularized form of the CN *ʔilm* (i.e. knowledge), as it must refer back to something specific within the context (either the linguistic context or the context of situation) and is therefore an entitive noun. Similarly an EN could be definite or indefinite as in 6a and 6b respectively

      5a *Alfikraato jaayyidaa* (The idea is fine)

      5b *Yaa laaha min fikraa* (what an idea!)

It is to be noted that in 6b the nunnation case ending diacritic is not phonologically explicit in the noun *"Fekra"* and is only made so when this noun is pos-modified by an explicit lexical adjective as 6c illustrates

     5c) Yaa laaha min fikraatin raiʔaa (what a wonderful idea!)

It is obvious that the semantic factor of referential scope is the key touchstone in differentiating between CNs and ENs in Arabic since they do not have the clear-cut syntactioc-semantic differentiating constraints their English counterparts have.

6.2 A Corpus-based Analysis of Lexical Transfer

In this section I do an investigation of the effect of the context on the conceptual configuration of the lexical items and how this effect in reflected in translation through the intermediation of the translator's dynamic bilingual lexicon. What is investigated here is whether, for instance, a generic concept will always retain its genericity in translation or whether the formal and the conceptual properties of lexical items converge or do they sometimes diverge for the sake of producing a communicative translation? In order to answer these questions six abstract concepts have been selected so that they represent different types of abstract concepts. The syntactic and semantic behavior of their nominal lexical realizations in the source language and the target language is investigated to throw some light on the interplay between text, conceptual structure and the lexicon in the translator's mind and how this is reflected in the final translational output. For this purpose, the United Nations bilingual corpus (English-Arabic bitexts) is used for the diversity of the translation registers it handles and the huge number of texts it contains. A sample of 10 corpus hits (i.e. stretches of text) for each of the six concepts has been randomly selected so that we have an aggregate of sixty-hit sample corpus (about 4000 words). Table (18) provides a classification of the occurrences of each concept on the conceptual and realization levels. On the realizational level it lists the entitive and conceptual nouns that are found for each concept in the 10-hit sample and their Arabic equivalents in the parallel corpus. On the conceptual level, table (18) sorts out the extensions and types of each concept and their lexical equivalents in the target language.

concept	Conceptual noun	Lxt	Entitive noun	lxt	extensions	lxt	types	lxt
science	Science (5)	العلم علم (٤)	1-Natural sciences 2-the sciences	١-العلـوم الطبيعية ٢- العلوم	1-information Science 2-science of ageing	١-علـم المعلومات ٢-علـم الشيخوخة	Natural sciences	العلوم الطبيعية
law	Law (4)	القانون					1-International Law (2) 2-Human trafficking law 3-International humanitarian law 4-Customary international law 5-Law of the sea	١-القانون الدولي ٢-قــانون الاتجــار بالبشر ٣- القانون الإنساني الدولي ٤-القـانون الـدولي العرفي ٥-قانون البحار
religion	Religion (4)	الدين	1-Religions (4) 2-Any religion	١-الأديان ٢-الدين			State religion	دين الدولة

collapse	collapse	انهيار				
mortality	Mortality (4)	(٣) الوفيـات (١)وفيـات		1-child mortality (2) 2-the mortality rate of children 3-infant mortality (1) 4-maternal Mortality (3)	١- معدل وفيات الأطفال ٢- معدل وفيات الأطفال ٣- وفيـــات الرضع ٤- الوفيـات النفاسية	
morbidity	1-morbidity (6)	المرض (٤) الاعتلال الإصابة بالأمراض		Maternal morbidity (4)	اعتلال الأمهات مراضـــة الأمومة الاعتلال أثناء النفاس الأمـــراض النفاسية	

Table (18): lexical transfer of six abstract concepts in a bilingual corpus

Science

The typical physical realization of the concept SCIENCE in the source language is the conceptual noun *science*. On the morpho-syntactic level the sciences is a plural entitive noun representing a collective term for the individual sciences. On the semantic level, *the sciences* is almost conceptually equivalent to the CN *science* in the ten-hit sample of science. This is because the former occurs in a context where it indicates a unitary conceptual entity rather than collective abstract entities as 1a below illustrates

1a) The spread of tension and conflict, the inability to find mutual and fair solutions for outstanding international issues, including the question of Palestine, as well as the profoundly unfair imbalance in the economy, the sciences and modern technologies, place international relations in a position of uncertainty

إن اتساع رقعة التوترات والنزاعات وعدم إيجاد حلول مشتركة ومنصفة للقضايا الدولية الراهنة، وخاصة منها القضية الفلسطينية، بالإضافة إلى ما يشهده العالم من تفاوت مجحف في موازين الاقتصاد والعلوم والتكنولوجيات الحديثة، يجعل العلاقات الدولية اليوم في وضع يبعث على القلق وعدم الاطمئنان،

The plural Arabic entitive noun Al?olwm, as the corpus hit 1a above shows, is a direct lexical transfer of the plural entitive noun *the sciences* and is conceptually equivalent to the concept SCIENCE.

The prototypical lexical transfer for the English CN *science* is the Arabic CN *Al?ilm* which is found in four cases out of five cases in which science occurs in the sample. *Ilm*, without a definite article, is an exception. It is found in the corpus as the lexical transfer of science in the phrase *a man of science*, which is rendered in Arabic as *Raagol ʔilm*. Information science and science of ageing are both extensions of science. There is no single-word term in English that can encapsulate the latter concept. For the former, however, there is the noun *informatics*. This is also true of Arabic where there is a single-word term for science of information, that is maaʔlwmaatyyaa while the extension science of ageing is physically realized by a combination of the generic concept name ilm+ the stative noun Alšaayxwxaa (ageing). Natural sciences, though a plural form of the entitive nominal *a natural science*, is semantically equivalent to the conceptual noun *natural science*, which is a type of science. This is because it occurs in a context where it indicates a unitary concept which is generic in scope:

1b) Ms. Zemene (Ethiopia) said that adoption of the draft resolution would contribute positively to the learning of young children and other students in the natural sciences throughout the world.

السيدة زيميني (إثيوبيا): قالت إن اعتماد مشروع القرار من شأنه أن يسهم على نحو إيجابي في مجال تعليم صغار الأطفال وسائر الطلبة فيما يتصل بالعلوم الطبيعية بكافة أنحاء العالم.

Therefore, *natural sciences* can be considered as a type of science from a semantic point of view. Similarly in Arabic, the nominal phrase Alʔolwm Altaabiʔyyaa, a plural form of the entitive noun ʔilm taabiʔi, plays the same conceptual role and is the direct lexical transfer of *natural sciences* as it occurs in 1b above.

Law

In the 10-hit random corpus sample chosen for law, the latter is realized as a conceptual noun in four hits out of 10. Its direct equivalent in the TL is the conceptual noun القانون Alqanwn. Since law extensions are inherently very limited, it is just natural that a random 10-hit sample tends to include a zero extension hit. No entitive noun realizations are found in this sample. The remaining six law occurrences are types of law, which are lexically realized in both languages in lexical conflations rather than single-word terms.

Religion

The concept RELIGION is lexically realized in English in the conceptual noun *religion* and in Arabic as the conceptual noun الدين Aldiin. This is evident from the four occurrences of *religion*, without modifiers or qualifying adjectives, and its translational equivalents in our sample bilingual corpus. In one of the four hits in which the conceptual noun *religion* occurs, it occurs in the nominal compound *freedom of religion*

3a) The Secretary-General has the honour to transmit to the members of the General Assembly the interim report of the Special Rapporteur on freedom of religion or belief, Asma Jahangir,

يتشرف الأمين العام بأن يحيل إلى أعضاء الجمعية العامة التقرير المؤقت المقدم من أسماء جهانجير، المقررة الخاصة المعنية بحرية الدين أو المعتقد

It is to be noted that *religion* in the above corpus hit does not imply the system concept *religion* as a whole but rather an action is involved. We can paraphrase the nominal compound as "freedom of exercising religious rituals and adopting religious beliefs". This intermarriage between the explicit system concept and an implicit action is rendered in Arabic in the same way by linking the SL noun to its direct CN in the TL without resorting to a paraphrase or an explanatory equivalent. *Religions*, which occurs four times, is a pluralized abstract entity, i.e. the plural form of an entitive noun. Unlike *sciences* in the science sample, *religions* is not conceptually equivalent to religion in the sample under investigation. For example, in 3b below

3b) The Arab Group calls for the promotion of dialogue, tolerance and understanding among civilizations, cultures, peoples and religions and for the criminalization of contempt to or defamation of religions or targeting their symbols,

وفـي هـذا الـسياق، تـدعو المجموعـة العربيـة إلـى تعزيـز الحـوار والتـسامح والتفـاهم بـين الحـضارات والثقافـات والـشعوب والأديـان والعمـل علـى تجريم ازدراء الأديان أو تشويهها أو المس برموزها

Religions are entities regarded collectively and do not represent a unitary concept for dialogue can take place between religious entities, which are lexically encapsulated collectively in the plural entitive noun *religions* and its direct Arabic equivalent الأديان

Now let us consider a different corpus hit:

3c) we have emphasized the need to address the root causes of terrorism and insisted that terrorism cannot and should not be associated with any religion, nationality, civilization or ethnic group.

.. شـددنا علـى ضـرورة معالجـة الأسـباب الجذريـة للإرهـاب، وأكـدنا علـى عـدم ربـط الإرهـاب بالـدين، والجنسية، والحضارة أو المجموعة العرقية

On the surface syntactic level, the noun phrase *any religion* represents an entitive nominal phrase. On a deeper conceptual-semantic level, it functions like a conceptual noun in this context. If we replace it by the conceptual noun *religion* we do not perceive any semantic difference. Apparently, the Arabic translator reached a similar decision and so opted for the conceptual noun Aldiin as a translation for the whole nominal phrase in this context rather than an equivalent entitive nominal phrase in the TL. Thus we can argue for translation as a detector of the conceptual content embedded in the formal structures of the source language.

Collapse

In the ten-hit corpus sample of The English noun *collapse*, we find that this noun has three meanings unified by the semantic spectrum of "falling down", i.e. the concrete basic sense of *falling down* itself, sudden *decrease* and *failure* as exemplified by the following sample corpus hits

4a) Israeli excavations in Silwan and the digging tunnels towards Al-Aqsa Mosque have caused the collapse of the ground in the United Nations Relief and Works Agency for Palestine Refugees in the Near East Girls School.

تسببت الحفريات الإسرائيلية في سلوان والأنفاق التي تحفر باتجاه المسجد الأقصى، في انهيار أرضية مدرسة البنات التابعة للأونروا.

4b) At the economic level, the impact of the financial crisis has had a fourfold effect: a plunge in financial and real-estate asset prices; a collapse in commodity prices

وعلى الصعيد الاقتصادي، كان للأزمة المالية تأثير له أربعة جوانب هي: هبوط أسعار الأصول المالية والعقارات؛ انهيار أسعار السلع الأساسية،

4c) The collapse of the Doha Round should be seen as a temporary setback.

إن انهيار جولة الدوحة ينبغي النظر إليه باعتباره نكسة مؤقتة

It can be argued that the second and third senses exemplified by 4b and 4c are a metaphoric extension of the first concrete sense exemplified by 4a. Such metaphoric extension represents some sort of a **cognitive metaphor**. A cognitive metaphor is a deviation from the traditional notion of the poetic metaphor and is assumed to be formed simply from direct contact with perceptual experience—without the intervention of the "figurative" level of language. The perceptual experience in the case of *collapse* is that of seeing a concrete structure *fall down* Thus, it is the case that the metaphoric is 'cognized' from the concrete through the universal faculty of concept-formation—not that the figurative is derived from the literal through the intermediation of language and the imagination.

It is not a coincidence that the Arabic deverbal noun *Inhyar* has the same three senses of the English noun *collapse*: one concrete sense and two metaphoric senses extended from the first one in much the same way. We can argue that the English noun *collapse* and its Arabic lexical equivalent *Inhyar* represent **a bilingual cognitive metaphor.** In 9 out of ten hits of the collapse sample translators favour the bilingual cognitive metaphor of "falling down, lexically realized in the Arabic noun *Inhyar*, over a lexical-word equivalent or a paraphrase. A lexical word equivalent such as Ixfaq (failure) for the third sense of failing pertains to a different semantic spectrum and a paraphrase like Hobwot mofaaj? (sudden decrease) for the second sense falls short of the metaphoric force of Inhyar.

Mortality

On the lexico-syntactic level, mortality is a conceptual noun realizing a state concept since it satisfies the formal criteria of a conceptual noun. On the semantic level, however, mortality entails an abstract entity since it implies "a death rate";it is a concept-related entity rather than a concept. Its logical extensions are all death rate values while its conceptual extensions are such extensions as infant mortality, child mortality, maternal mortality where the central identification criterion is the persons represented by the death toll. This is why the usual translation, as shown in table (18), of the conceptual noun *mortality*, when it stands alone, is the plural entitive noun waafaayat which literally means "deaths". In the nominal compounds that lexically encapsulate the extensions, the entitive element of the concept i.e. rate, is made lexically explicit in the Arabic translations.

The extension *maternal mortality* represents a special case as far the role played by the text in the lexical transfer of conceptual content is concerned. The term *maternal mortality* in World Health Organization texts usually refers to death that happens in the postpartum period. This period is known in Arabic as Nifaas. UN translators usually ignore the lexical meaning of the adjective *maternal* and concentrate on the textual meaning, translating the nominal compound as *wafayat Nifasya*, literally:post-partum deaths. In its own right, post-partum mortality is a type of mortality, not an extension since the adjective post-partum represents an external overspecifying feature other than the central identification criterion. Thus the interaction between the translator's interpretive mind and the text can change an extension in the SL into a type in the TL as far as lexical transfer is concerned. Though this is a case of overcontexualization by the translator, it shows how text pragmatics can affect the conceptual configuration of lexical items.

Morbidity

In the ten-hit sample selected for morbidity from the UN English-Arabic bitexts, it is to be noticed that whenever the CN *morbidity* is used in a generic sense, unqualified by adjectives and unfettered by being lexically conflated in nominal compounds, the generic Arabic term maaraad (illness) is used as its direct equivalent. This is usually the case in titles of programs and brief statements that give a general idea about a subject, as is illustrated in 6a below:

6a) General debate on national experience in population matters: health, morbidity, mortality and development.

] مناقشة عامـة بشـأن الخبـرة الوطنيـة فـي المسائل السكانية: الصحة والمرض والوفيات والتنمية.

The noiminal phrase *Alisabaa bilmaaraad* (being affected by illness), which is the equivalent provided by one translator for one of the four generic occurrences of morbidity is just a paraphrase of the Arabic generic term *maaraad*. When the conceptual noun *morbidity* is qualified by an adjective, we find that the translator resorts to a more specific term. Let us consider the following corpus-hit

6b) Induced abortion increases short-term mortality and morbidity and long-term morbidity. It damages the reproductive health of women

ويؤدي الإجهاض العمـدي إلى زيادة معدلات الوفيات والاعتلال فـي الأجل القصير، وإلـى زيـادة معدلات الاعتلال في الأجل الطويل، كمـا أنـه يضر بالصحة الإنجابية للمرأة بسبب

Ali?tilal, which means in Arabic extreme illness, can be considered as a type of maaraad (illness) which introduces a peripheral overspecification criterion to the generic concept, i.e. that of intensity. Thus a generic concept in English can be rendered as a type in Arabic depending on the context.

The four occurrences of *maternal morbidity* represent an extension of *morbidity* in which the central identification criterion, as in the case of mortality, is the person affected by illness. In the lexical transfer of this extension, sometimes the translator resorts to the lexical meaning and produces a translational equivalent in which the CIC is made lexically explicit as in 6c

6c) This statement is specifically concerned with the elimination of preventable maternal mortality and morbidity.

ويتعلق هذا البيان تحديداً بالتخلص مما يمكن توقيه من وفيات ومراضة الأمومة.

Where the highlighted translation equivalent miradaat Alomwmaa (literally: motherhood illness) is a direct translation in which the two lexical components of the SL compound maternal+morbidity are made explicit in the translation.

In other cases the translator resorts to a context-based type as a translational equivalent:

6d) Unsafe abortion is a major contributor to maternal mortality and morbidity, accounting for nearly 50, 000 women's and girls' deaths annually, according to the latest available estimates from WHO.

أما الإجهاض غير المأمون فهو من العناصر الرئيسية المتسببة في الوفيات والأمراض النفاسية، وهو مسؤول عن حوالي ٥٠ ٠٠٠ حالة وفاة في صفوف النساء والفتيات سنويا، حسب أحدث التقديرات المتاحة الصادرة عن منظمة الصحة العالمية.

The difference in the lexical transfer of *maternal morbidity* between 6c) and 6d) can be attributed to the fact that 6c is a general statement about the elimination of maternal mortality and morbidity, which induced the translator to consider only the linguistic meaning of the lexical items. This triggered direct links between the SL lexical items and their ready lexical equivalents in the translator's bilingual mental lexicon. The excerpt in 6d is specialized in nature and includes primes that trigger a medical lexical equivalent, that is the type Amra<u>d</u> nifasyyaa (post-partum diseases).

Conclusion

The study of abstract nouns in the bilingual mental lexicon has enabled us to differentiate between logical extension and semantic extension. The former refers to all members belonging under a category while the latter refers only to those ones that are related to the concept core. This conceptualistic approach to lexical semantics can enhance the rather too general classification of paradigmatic relations between lexical items into hyponomy, meronomy, hyperonymy, synonymy etc. While the traditional paradigm in lexical semantics sets the lexical items in neat vertical and horizontal relations to each other, it lacks conceptual refinement since it fails to relate each lexical unit to a concept core and an identification criterion whereby the semantic componential properties can be judged to be central or peripheral according to their relatedness to the internal kernel of the concept or its periphery. This kernel and periphery can be arrived at by using the analytic tools suggested by the study. Gaining such conceptual precision in lexical semantics proves to be useful in analyzing conceptual transfer of lexical items in translation. If there is always something lost and something gained in translation, what is lost or gained can only be identified by studying the interactions between the componential properties of concepts and the associative and semantic priming of the text and context. The aim of rehabilitating the classical view of concepts was to minimize the inherent fuzziness of concepts. In trying to reach a theoretical model that helps us understand the conceptual semantics of translation, we find ourselves already encumbered by the fuzziness caused by the text. The fact that we can have a model that constrains inherent fuzziness of concepts can help us better understand the interactions between the constituent properties of concepts and the text and context at hand and how these are reflected and re-enacted in translation.

Vis-à-vis lexical and conceptual processing in the bilingual mental lexicon, the current study provides a hybrid model that encompasses the shared and separate concept hypothesis in lexical transfer.

The fact that the bilingual test results converge with the monolingual results of tests conducted with Arabic native speakers and English native speakers separately attests to this hybridization. The bilingual finding that mean response times for type translation were higher than those scored for extensions and superordinates is perfectly consistent with the monolingual finding that in both English and Arabic item production tasks extensions are listed far more frequently than types and superordinates. In addition, typicality scores of types are less than those of extensions. It is clear from the autonomous model exhibited by the monolingual task results and shared model exhibited by the bilingual task results that analytic concepts are given processing priority both in the bilingual mind and the monolingual mind over synthetic ones.

This hybrid model also integrates the lexical mediation and conceptual mediation hypothesis suggested by Kroll (1993). Kroll suggested that translation from the first language to the second language is hypothesized to be conceptually mediated, whereas translation from the second language to the first is hypothesized to be lexically mediated. It is our contention here that whether translation is conceptually mediated or lexically mediated depends on the context. An example of conceptual mediation is when a generic SL term is translated into a specific term in the TL. When an entitive noun, for instance, is translated as a conceptual noun in the target language, this is an example of lexical mediation.

In conclusion, formal equivalence in many cases converges with conceptual equivalence. In other cases, they do not and conceptual equivalence takes priority. The translator in such a case finds himself in a position where he has to search for a form which is conceptually equivalent though not formally identical to the source word.

Feasibility of the study

The applied feasibility of this study can be most evident in the field of bilingual lexicography. The bilingual lexicographer can select a generic equivalent that takes the lexical meaning into consideration and then list other equivalents which are domain-specific, based on a systematic corpus investigation of the frequency of deviations from the core lexical meaning as dictated by the contexts under investigation. Also he can make use of the prototypical theory by selecting a prototypical lexical equivalent that shares the semantic properties of all senses of an SL polysemous lexical item. This prototypical equivalent can be used when a translator fails to find the exact partial equivalent for a specific collocational occurrence. For example, the Arabic verb yadrib can be a prototypical equivalent for the verb *beat* since it can replace such partial equivalents as yaqraa (beat a drum) or *yokhfiq* (beat an egg).

Notes

Chapter 1

1   Aitchison, 2003: p.10
2   Singleton, 2000: p161
3   Bonin, 2003: IV).
4   (Bonin, 2003: IV).
5   (Zelnick, 1990:p.1).
6   (Aitchison, 2003: P.9).
7   "(ibid: p.7).
8   (Cotteril, 1998: P.481).
9   (James, 1981:P.615, Aitchison, 2002:P.19).
10   "(Aitchison, 2003: p.19)
11   Balolta&Chumbley, 1984
12   (McNamara, 2005 p.1).

13   (Ludovic Ferrand and Boris New, 2003:p.26)
14   (Aitchison, 2003:p.10).
15   ibid, 2002: p.19)
16   (Aitchison, 2003:p.12)
17   (Hudson, 1983:p.74)
18   (Fodor, 1981:P.287).
19   (Aitchison, 2003.p.14)

20   (ibid:p.14).
21   (Schreuder and Flores D'acrais, 1996 p.411)
22   (Murphy, 2004: P.204)
23   (Kempson, 1979;Palmer, 1997)
24   (Murphy, 2004:P.388).
25   (Murphy, 2004:p.385)
26   (Schreuder and Flores D'acrais, 1996:p.409).

27 (Murphy, 2004:390).
28 (ibid:p.389):
29 Garrod and Sanford (1977, p.16)
30 (Aitchison, 2003:p.25, citing Marslen-Wilson, 1989b)

31 (Handke, 1995:P.113).
32 (ibid p.15).
33 (ibid p15-16)
34 (Handke, 1995:P.41).
35 (Garnham, 1985:188).
36 Singleton (2000:p.170)
37 (Singleton, 2000:p.173-174).
38 (Baetens, 1986)
39 (Robert Schreuder&Bert Weltens, 1993:P.6).
40 "(Robert Schreuder&Bert Weltens, 1993:P.7)
41 (Genesee, 1978:P.19)
42 (Baetens, 1986:p.3).

43 (Baetens, 1986:P.4)

44 (Houston, 1972: 203-25)
45 (Jarvis, 1998:P.26 citing Paradis, 1994, 1997)
46 (Lakoff, 1987:P.455)
47 (Jarvis, 1998:P.23).
48 (ibid.P.24)
49 (ibid.P.27).
50 "(Dong, 2005)
51 ibid
52 "(Kroll, 1993:P.52).

53 (De Groot, 1993:P.32)
54 (Kroll, 1993:P.64)
55 (Lupker, 1984; Kroll, 1993)
56 Shwanenflugel and Rey 1986:p.605-618)
57 (De Groot, 1991:p.101-123).
58 (Weinreich, 1974)
59 (potter et al., 1984:p.23)
60 (De Groot, 1993:P.27)
61 (ibid P.46).
62 (Bell, 1995:p.26).
63 (ibid, 1995:p.15)
64 Kroll, 1993, Sondgrass, 1993
65 Smyth et al., 1994:p.93.
66 Bell, 1995:P.48

[67]   ibid P.49
[68]   Larson, 1997:p.55
[69]   ibid:p.55
[70]   Bell, 1995.
[71]   ibid, 1995, P.243-245.
[72]   ibid P.246
[73]   ibid P.246
[74]   ibid.p.246.
[75]   Kempson, 1979:p.18, Bell, 1995:p.91
[76]   Baddeley, 2005:p.1; Bell, 1995:255
[77]   Bell, 1995:234
[78]   Baker, 2009:p.189
[79]   Green, 1993:P.257.
[80]   Larson, 1997:P.154.

[81]   ibid.P.153-72

[82]   Beekman and Callow, 1974:185-86.
[83]   Schmid (2000, p.4
[84]   ibid:P.10
[85]   ibid:P.13
[86]   (ibid P.54)
[87]   Heyvaert, Lisebet, 2006
[88]   Lakoff, 1987:p.58
[89]   "Kroll, 1993:p.64.
[90]   De Groot, 1993:p.41.

[91]   ibid.P.41.
[92]   De Groot, 1992b:p.18
[93]   Larson, 1997:156-57
[94]   Baker, 2011:p.24
[95]   Baker, 2011:p.38.

[96]   Anani, 1992:10-33.
[97]   ibid p.13
[98]   ibid P.26
[99]   (ibid:p11).

Chapter 2

[100]   St.Thomas, de triniate, q.5, a.3

[101]   St.Thomas, de triniate, q.5, a.3.

[102] Frisch, 1969.p.151

[103] Aristotle, Categories.c4
[104] Kant, 1781.Critique of pure reason
[105] Matindale, 1981:p.5-6
[106] Brandon, 2003, askaphilosopher.co.uk
[107] Frisch, 1969.
[108] Frisch, 1969.p.143
[109] Frisch, 1969.p.165.
[110] Smith&Medin, 1981.p.25.
[111] Smith&Medin, 1981: p.15.
[112] ibid.p.18
[113] ibid p.20.
[114] Smith&Medin, 1981, osherson et al.1990, Murphy.2004
[115] Murphy, 2004:p.202
[116] ibid:p.18.
[117] Murphy (2004.
[118] Rips, Shoben and Smith, 1973:1-20
[119] Rosch&Mervis 1975:p.573
[120] Barsalou, 1987, Rosch, 1976.
[121] Hampton, 1982:151-164
[122] Smith&Medin, 1981.p.143
[123] ibid:p.26

Chapter 3

[124] Lucy, 2001:p.42.

Chapter 4

[125] (Metcalfe, J., & Shimamura, A. P., 1994)
[126] L.T.FGamut, 1991:p.16
[127] Peterson, 1973:p.121.
[128] Katz, 1966:p.181
[129] Davidson, 1979, Kempson, 1989
[130] Kempson, 1989:p.13.
[131] cf.Lakoff, p.85
[132] Talmy, 2000:p.43
[133] Fodor, Jerry A. (1983).

Bibliography

1. Aitchison, Jean. 2003. Words in the Mind: an introduction to the Mental Lexicon. 3d edn. Australia. Blackwell Publishing.
2. Anani, Muhammed. 1992. Fan Al-Tarjama (Art of Translation). Cairo. Longman.
3. Anglin, J.M. 1977. Word, object, and conceptual development. New York:Norton.
4. Baddley, Alan D. 2005:Essentials of Human Memory. Taylor &Francais e-library.www.ebookstore.tandf.co.uk
5. Baker, Mona &Saldanha Gabriel. 2009. Routledge Encyclopedia of translation studies. 2d edt. Abingdon. Routledge.
6. Baker, Mona. 2011:In other words. Taylor &Francais e-library. www.ebookstore.tandf.co.uk
7. Balota, D.A and Chumbley, J.I. 1984. Are lexical decisions a good measure of lexical access? The role of word-frequency in the neglected decision stage. Journal of experimental psychology: Human perception and performance. New York. APA and Affiliated Journals.
8. Barsalou, L.W 1987. The instability of graded structure:Implications for the nature of concepts. In U.Neisser (Ed.), Concepts and Conceptual Development:Ecological and Intellectual Factors in Categorization. Cambridge: Cambridge University Press.

9. Bassnet, Susan. 2005:Translation Studies (new Accents). Taylor &Francais e-library.www.ebookstore.tandf.co.uk

10. Beardsmore, Hugo Baetens, 1986. Bilingualism:Basic Principles- 2nd ed. Bank House. England. Multilingual matters Ltd.

11. Bell, Roger T 1995. translation and translating:theory and practice. Essex. UK. Longman Group.

12. Berlin, Isaiah et al. 1978, Concepts and Categories. 8th edn. New Jersey. Princeton University Press.

13. Bonin, Patrick2003, The Mental lexicon "some words to talk about words", New York.: New York Publishers, Inc,

14. Callanan, M.A. 1985. How parents label objects for young children:The role of input in the acquisition of category hierarchies. Child Development., 56. Society for Research in Child Development. Ann Arbor, Michigan

15. Collins, A., and M.R. Quillian. 1969. Retrieval time from semantic memory. Journal of verbal learning and verbal behavior. New York and London, Academic Press.

16. Corter, J.E. and Gluck, M.A. 1992. Explaining basic categories:Feature predicability and information. Psychological Bulletin, 111. Washington DC. American Psychological Association.

17. Cotteril, R 1998. Enchanted looms:Conscious Networks in Brains and Computers. Cambridge. Cambridge University Press.

18. Davidson, Donald. 2001 Inquiries into Truth and Meaning, 2nd edition. Oxford: Oxford University Press

19. De Groot, Annette M.B. 1993. Word-type effects in Bilingual Processing Tasks:support for a Mixed Representational System. The Bilingual Lexicon. Amsterdam. John Benjamins Publishing Co.

20. DONG, YANPING 2005, Shared and separate meanings in the bilingual mental lexicon. Bilingualism: Language and Cognition 8 (3). Cambridge University Press.

21. Fodor, J.A. 1981. Representations:Philosophical Essays on the Foundations of Cognitive Science. Cambridge, MA:MIT Press.

22. Fodor, Jerry A. (1983). *Modularity of Mind: An Essay on Faculty Psychology*. Cambridge, Mass.: MIT Press

23. Frisch, Joseph C. 1969. Extension and Comprehension in Logic. New York. Philosophical Library.

24. Garnham, Alan, 1985. Psycholingustics. London: Methuen& Co.

25. Garrod, S. and Sanford, A 1977. Interpreting anaphoric relations: The integration of semantic information while reading. Journal of verbal learning and verbal behavior. New York and London. Academic Press.

26. Genesee, G., Hamers, J., Lambert, W.E., E., Mononen, L., Seitz, M., & Starck, R. 1978. Language processing in bilinguals. Brain and Language

27. Halliday. M.A.k 1978. Language as a social Semiotic: The social Interpretation of Language and Meaning. London. Longman.

28. Hampton, J.A. 1982. A demonstration of intransitivity in natural categories. Cognition, 12. Heslington. UK

29. Handke, Jurgen 1995, The Structure of the Lexicon;human versus machine, Berlin. Walter de Gruyter& Co.

30. Heyvaert, Lisebet (2006), book Review of Schmid's abstract nouns as conceptual shells, FWO-Vlaanderen & University of Leuven, Angenita Connect.

31. Hudson, R. 1984a. Invitation to Linguistics. London:Martin Robinson.

32. Houston, SH 1972, **Bilingualism: Naturally Acquired Bilingualism, A Survey of Psycholinguistics**. The Hague: Mouton, Huerta

33. J. Vrin 1947 Prophyry's Isagoge. Paris: Librairie Philosophique, Trans. J.tricot

34. James, William. 2007. The Principles of Psychology, vol 2. Cambridge, MA:Harvard University Press.

35. Katz, 1966. The Philosophy of Language. New York, Harper & Row.

36. Kempson, Ruth. m, Semantic Theory, 1989, 5th edn, Oxford. Alden Press.

37. Keon MC (editor). 1941: The basic Works of Aristotle. New York. Random House.

38. Kroll, Judith F. 1993. Accessing Conceptual Representations for Words in a Second Language. The Bilingual Lexicon. Amsterdam. John Benjamins Publishing Co.

39. Lakoff, George. 1989. Metaphors we live by Michigan. Michigan University Press.

40. Larsen 1997. Meaning-based translation: A Guide to cross-linguistic equivalence. 2nd edt. Lanham. University Press of America.

41. Lucy, Niall 2001. Beyond Semiotics:Text, Culture and Technology. New York. Continuum.

42. Ludovic Ferrand & Boris. 2003 Schweizerische Zeitschrift Für Psychologie Und Ihre Andwendungen. New Psychologie. New York. Nova Publishers.

43. Kant, 1781. Critique of pure reason, Meiklejohn translation (2003 edition) Project Gutenberg Literary Archive Foundation, Oxford

44. Lupker, S. J. (1984). Semantic priming without association: a second look. Journal of Verbal Learning and Verbal Behavior, 23. New York and London. Academic Press

45. Matindale, Cole 1981. Cognition and Consciousness 3rd edn. CA, USA, Dorsey Press.

46. McCloskey, M.E Cluckseberg, S 1978. Natural Categories:Well-defined or fuzzy sets? Memory and Cognition, 6. Austin. Texas

47. Mcnamara, Timothy P. 2005. Semantic priming: perspectives from memory and word recognition. 1st edn. NY.Taylor&Francis Group.

48. Metcalfe, J., & Shimamura, A. P. 1994. Metacognition: knowing about knowing. Cambridge, MA: MIT Press.

49. Miller, G.A., and P.N. Johnson-Laird. 1976. Language and perception. Cambridge, Mass.: Harvard University Press.

50. Murphy, Gregory. 2004, The big book of concepts. Mit Press

51. Nelson, K. 1974. Concept, Word, and sentence: Interrelations in acquisition and development. Psychological Review. Washington, D.C., the American Psychological Association

52. Osherson, D.N., Stern, J.Wilkie, O.Stob, M., and Smith, E.D. 1991. Default Probability. Cognitive Science. Beijing. The International Association For Cognitive Science.

53. P. Bazzi et al. 1953 Aquinas, St.Thomas. "De Potentia" in Quaestiones Disputate. Ed Taurini:Marietti.

54. Palmer, F.R, 1997, Semantics, 2d edn. Cambridge. Cambridge University Press.

55. Potter, M.C., So, K.F., Von Eckardt, B., & Feldman, L. (1984). Lexical and conceptual representation in beginning and proficient bilinguals. Journal of Verbal Learning and Verbal Behavior, 23(1). New York and London. Academic Press.

56. Peterson, Philip L. 1973. Concepts and language . . . An essay in generative semantics and the philosophy of language, The Hague. Janua linguarum. Series minor, Mouton de Gruyter.

57. Rips, L.J., Shoben, E.J., and E.Smith. 1973. Semantic distance and the verification of semantic relations. Journal of Verbal Learning and Verbal Behaviour. Vol 6. New York and London. Academic Press.

58. Robert Schreuder&Bert Weltens, 1993. The Bilingual Lexicon. Amsterdam. John Benjamins Publishing Co.

59. Rosch, E., and C.B Mervis. 1975. Family resemblance studies in the internal structure of categories. Journal of Cognitive Psychology. Pennsilvenya State University.

60. Saussure, Ferdinand de. (2002) *Écrits de linguistique générale* (edition prepared by Simon Bouquet and Rudolf Engler), Paris: Gallimard. I. English translation: *Writings in General Linguistics*, Oxford: Oxford University Press.

61. Schmid, Hans-Jörg 2000. *English Abstract Nouns as Conceptual Shells. From Corpus to Cognition.* Berlin: Mouton de Gruyter

62. Schreuder and Flores D'acrais. 1996, lexical representation and process, Masschusetts. MIT Press.

63. Singleton, David, 2000 Language and the Lexicon. New York. Oxford University Press.

64. Smith, Edward E&. Medin, Douglas L. 1981. Categories and Concepts. London. Harvard University Press.

65. Smyth et al., 1994:Cognition in Action. Hove. UK. Earlbaum Associates.

66. Snodgrass, J.G. (1993). "Translating versus picture naming: similarities and differences." In: R. Schreuder and B. Weltens (Eds.), *The bilingual lexicon*. Amsterdam/Philadelphia: Benjamins.

67. Jarvis, Scott. 1998. Conceptual transfer in the interlingual lexicon. Bloomington, Ind.: Indiana University Linguistics Club Publications.

68. Weinreich, Uriel. 1974. *Language in Contact*. The Hague: Mouton

69. Zelnick, Lawrence. 1990. Buchholz, Ester S. Psychoanalytic. Psychology, Vol 7(1), Academic Press. New York and London.

Appendix I

List of Abbreviations

CN = Conceptual Noun
EN = Entitive noun
TL = Target Language
SL = Source Language
CIC = Central Identification Criterion
PIC = Peripheral Identification Criterion
RT = Response Time
TS = Typicality Score
PR = Physical Realization
AR = Abstract Realization
AE = Abstract Entity
GE = Generic Equivalent
LXT = Lexical Transfer
GN = Generic Noun
Ext = Extension
Real = Realization
Ms = millisecond

Appendix II

Phonetic Notation of the Arabic Writing System

Arabic letter	Transcription symbol
ء	ʔ
آ	a
ا	e̱
آ	ö
ى	i̱
ؤ	o̱
ب	b
ت	t
ث	θ
ج	j
ح	ẖ
خ	x
د	d
ذ	ő

ر	r
ز	z
س	s
ش	š
ص	s̲
ض	d̲
ط	t̲
ظ	d̲̲
ع	ʕ
غ	**M**
ف	f
ق	q
ك	k
ل	l
م	m
ن	n
ه	h
و	w
ي	y
ٓ	aa
ٖ	i
ٔ	O
ٱ	Ö